Arctic Airmen

The RAF in Spitsbergen and North Russia, 1942

ARCTIC AIRMEN

THE RAF IN SPITSBERGEN AND NORTH RUSSIA, 1942

by

Ernest Schofield & Roy Conyers Nesbit

Foreword by

Sir Alexander Glen, KBE, DSC

SPELLMOUNT
Staplehurst

British Library Cataloguing in Publication Data:
A catalogue record for this book is available
from the British Library

Copyright © Ernest Schofield & Roy Conyers Nesbit 1987, 2005

ISBN 1-86227-291-3

First published in 1987 by
William Kimber & Co Ltd

This edition first published in the UK in 2005 by
Spellmount Limited
The Village Centre
Staplehurst
Kent TN12 0BJ

Tel: 01580 893730
Fax: 01580 893731
E-mail: enquiries@spellmount.com
Website: www.spellmount.com

1 3 5 7 9 8 6 4 2

Printed in Great Britain by
T.J. International Ltd
Padstow, Cornwall

For Tim

Contents

List of Maps and Diagrams

List of Illustrations

Foreword
by

Sir Alexander Glen, KBE, DSC

For many centuries, the Arctic Seas had known only peace. True, skirmishes between Dutch and English whalers troubled the Spitsbergen bays in the 17th and 18th centuries, but these were limited local affairs and strategic war was unknown.

World War Two brought abrupt change. The sinking of *Hood* by *Bismarck* in the Denmark Strait was the first act in the opening of a new and bitter theatre of operations. Then came the build-up of German naval and air power in north Norway. When the German onslaught on Soviet Russia took momentum, it might have seemed that the gate was closed on any western attempt to supply her new ally by the Northern Seas.

The Allies took a little time to recognise the new strategic situation. Information on the Arctic Seas was scant enough and almost non-existent about the sea ice, particularly in the narrow and vulnerable channels between North Cape of Norway and Spitsbergen. Flying had been restricted to some four exploratory flights. In any case, the RAF had no aircraft capable of reaching the higher latitudes until it began to receive delivery of the Catalina flying boats. Most important of all, the fortunes of war in 1941 and 1942 were such that survival more than occupied the minds of most. There was little to encourage long-term gambles, or indeed anything beyond the problems of the day.

A few highly-placed officers thought differently. The Assistant Chief of Naval Staff, Rear Admiral E.J.P. Brind, and the Director of Operations Division (Home), Captain J.A.S. Eccles, were at one with the director of Naval Intelligence, Rear Admiral J.H. Godfrey, in assessing the appalling problems the northern sea route would pose. In Coastal Command, Air Chief Marshal Sir Philip Joubert, ably backed by an outstanding Senior Air Staff Officer, Air Vice Marshal G.B.A. Baker, had already perceived the contribution that the new 'very long range' Catalinas might make.

If the Falklands campaign was fought at long range, just as extreme were the air and naval operations of 1942/43 over the Arctic

Sea. The most critical sector passed through enemy air space and, indeed, what could have been enemy-dominated sea space. The channels between North Cape, Norway, Bear Island and Spitsbergen were especially critical and Spitsbergen itself was a pivotal point.

Allied policy accordingly was to deprive the enemy of the use of Spitsbergen provided this could be done by a small mobile force with minimal demand on the war effort elsewhere. Germany's interest, as this book shows, was significantly different. Logistically they felt stretched far enough in north Norway itself, and their compelling need in Spitsbergen was for weather stations. It was perhaps hesitancy on the part of the German High Command, shown especially in their failure to deploy effectively their capital ships concentrated in northern Norway, that was to make it possible for the Allies to maintain the northern sea route to Russia, despite appallingly heavy losses in June 1942.

The Allies' solution was a small land force of some 80 Norwegians, mostly ex-miners from Spitsbergen, hardy, experienced in polar survival, skilled ski runners, men who regarded the Arctic as their home. How they turned initial disaster into outstanding success is part of the story told in this book.

The other and central part is how one Catalina of 210 Squadron, commanded by Flight Lieutenant D.E. Healy, DSO, and navigated by Flight Lieutenant E. Schofield, DFC, made this possible. In the course of three 24-hour flights in seven days in May 1942, they made contact with the survivors of the original force, re-armed them, then evacuated their wounded, and finally provided the communication link which enabled survival to be turned into attack.

In January 1987, 45 years later, Ernest Schofield, Ronald Martin (the second pilot) and I attended the opening in North Norway of the Norwegian Defence Museum's exhibition of these events. It included the German activities in the Arctic, including the achievements of the Luftwaffe weather squadrons, as well as those of the Allies. It is good that there should be displayed throughout Norway such a record of how a tiny Norwegian garrison held Spitsbergen, even surviving bombardment of the heavy ships of the German Navy, including *Tirpitz*. It is also important historically that the contribution made by 'Tim' Healy and his crew, which was vital to the Allied recovery as shown in this narrative, is suitably included in these exhibitions.

The consequences of these events, however, are both greater and longer-lasting than any of us would have thought 45 years ago. Not only did Spitsbergen remain a free Norwegian territory throughout the war years, it remains so today. Spitsbergen's pivotal position has a new and contemporary significance in the context of the massive concentration of Soviet power in Murmansk.

Acknowledgements

We are very grateful for the help given to us, when researching the material for this book, by officials and staff at the following organisations:

Aeroplane Monthly, International Publishing Corp., Sutton.
Commonwealth War Graves Commission, Maidenhead.
Forsvarsmuseet, Oslo.
General Dynamics, Convair Division, California.
Imperial War Museum, Lambeth.
Ministry of Defence, Air Historical Branch, Holborn.
Ministry of Defence, Naval Historical Branch, Fulham.
Public Record Office, Kew.
Royal Air Force Museum, Hendon.
Royal Geographical Society, Kensington Gore.
Royal Greenwich Observatory, Herstmonceaux.
Royal Norwegian Embassy, Pall Mall.
Scott Polar Research Institute, Cambridge.

Our thanks are also due to those who generously contributed their detailed recollections of the events related in this book:

Sir Alexander R. Glen, KBE, DSC.
Flight Lieutenant Ronald Martin, RAFVR.
Squadron Leader Reginald W. Witherick, RAFVR.
Flight Lieutenant George W. Adamson, RAFVR.

We should like to express our gratitude to Mrs Jean Podlipny and Mr Brian Healy for contributing their recollections of the early life of their brother, Flight Lieutenant Dennis E. Healy, DSO.

For the accounts of the German weather airmen in the Arctic, we have drawn on the research and writing carried out by Herr Franz Selinger, and we are very grateful to him and his colleagues for authorising us to make use of records and photographs.

For translation from Norwegian and German records, we have benefited from the assistance kindly given by Mrs I. Moorcraft, Mr N. Wajsmel, and by the staff of Forsvarsmuseet in Oslo.

Mr Harry R. Moyle was most generous in letting us have the

results of his researches into the fates of the Hampdens of 144 Squadron during their flights to North Russia.

We should also like to thank Mr Gordon Railton and Mr Michael H. Nesbit for assistance with copying and improving old photographs, and Mr Peter Nesbit for designing the cover.

Crown copyright material in the Public Record Office is reproduced by permission of Her Majesty's Stationery Office.

Finally, we should like to express our gratitude to families and friends for their tolerance and help while we were engaged on writing this book, in a period when unexpected problems caused long delays.

Authors' Note

Although the narrative of this book is written in the first person by one author, Ernest Schofield, it is in fact a joint work with another author, Roy Conyers Nesbit.

In October 1984, Ernest Schofield attended a talk given by Air Chief Marshal Sir Lewis Hodges, KCB, CBE, DSO, DFC. During a discussion afterwards, Ernest Schofield mentioned that he had flown on a number of special flights to Spitsbergen and North Russia, and still had in his possession several navigation logs written in the air while engaged on this Arctic flying.

Sir Lewis Hodges was interested enough to approach Air Commodore Henry Probert, MBE, the head of the Air Historical Branch of the Ministry of Defence. In turn, Air Commodore Probert suggested to Roy Conyers Nesbit that he should take a look at this material, particularly since it included an account of the first attempt by the RAF to fly to the North Pole.

Ernest Schofield and Roy Conyers Nesbit combined forces to research the background to these flights, at the Air Historical and Naval Historical Branches of the MoD, the Imperial War Museum, the Public Record Office, the Royal Geographical Society, the Scott Polar Institute, and many other places. They also obtained from sources in Germany the Luftwaffe side of this story. Above all, they traced several of the participants in this dramatic conflict.

Thus, the navigation logs provided an accurate basis, but only a starting point, for this little-known story.

CHAPTER ONE

Reluctant Volunteer

Many RAF aircrews were required to fly on hazardous missions during the war. Some were aimed at specific and important targets with precise objectives, such flights normally being part of a squadron effort in which many aircrews took part. Occasionally, however, some tasks had to be carried out as lone operations, with little advance preparation. I was a member of an aircrew required to undertake such a series of flights, one of which probably ranks as among the most unusual of the war – a reconnaissance flight to the North Pole.

At a time when advances in technology have brought precision to air navigation and airlines make regular scheduled flights at high latitudes, such a task may now seem fairly inconsequential. However, for a squadron aircrew to be singled out and expected to tackle such a project in the circumstances of 1942 was unprecedented, especially since we ourselves were required to solve all the problems that were entailed.

The polar flight was associated with a Norwegian expedition from Britain to Spitsbergen. The original intention was that Coastal Command would play only an ancillary role in the operation. In the event, however, our aircrew became directly involved and other squadron aircrews also had to take part. These flights, and the impact that they made on the operation, constitute the main events in this narrative.

Immediately after the adventures in Spitsbergen and the attempt at the polar flight, a detachment of the squadron moved to North Russia to take part in an operation to protect convoys taking military supplies to our Allies on the Eastern Front. These Russian sorties provided further experience of Arctic flying and led to the tragedy that befell our aircrew.

All these northern patrols were long flights, many of them over 24 hours in duration, crossing the apparently endless expanses of Arctic seas in flying conditions that tested human endurance to the limit. In themselves, they are worthy of being placed on record. But of even

21

greater significance is the recognition deserved by the men who made them possible.

The polar flight and the Spitsbergen sorties were exceptional, as was the captain chosen to undertake them. It was my privilege to be the navigator of his crew. This resulted partly from selection, but it could also be attributed to some accidents of fate. In fact, my position in the aircrew was somewhat anomalous since, although I volunteered for flying duties, it was expediency which prompted me rather than a wish to see action in the air.

I was born in 1916 of Yorkshire parents, Benjamin and Alice Schofield, in the moorland town of Penistone. Four years later, my family moved to Derby where I followed my elder brother to the municipal secondary school, which was later renamed Bemrose School. My strongest subject in the lower school was mathematics, but by the time I entered the sixth form geography occupied first place. This brought a scholarship to St John's College, Cambridge, where I changed my preference once again and read economics, gaining an honours degree in due course.

Cambridge provided an environment where hard work could be combined with a very enjoyable life style. Two hours rowing on the Cam every afternoon improved physical fitness. This offset the strain of grappling with the theories of John Maynard Keynes, the most eminent economist of the time. Listening to such great masters enlarged my appreciation of what seemed to be the unlimited capacity of some human intellects. We learned how to tackle the unknown and gained confidence in our ability to achieve results from logical analysis. The subject matter was to have little bearing on wartime activities, but it is probable that these studies engendered an attitude of mind which helped me in subsequent events.

It was extremely difficult to find a job in the inter-war years of depression. My solution was to stay on for a fourth year at Cambridge, reading history, until I was old enough to take the competitive entrance examinations for the Civil Service. I took up my first post in January 1939, in the Department of Inland Revenue. This turned out to be an occupation which, on the outbreak of war eight months later, carried 'reservation' from military service. This was no embarrassment to me. I was sure that I possessed no latent military talent, and I would have been quite content to make my contribution to the war effort as a civilian.

The rapid advance of the Wehrmacht across Europe changed my status. 'Dereservation' of my occupation brought the option of waiting for conscription or volunteering for the service of my choice. The Army did not appeal at all, for it carried the stigma of trench warfare in my estimation. The Royal Navy was also a non-starter, for I suffered from sea-sickness. On the other hand, the aircrew branch of the Royal Air Force seemed to offer some attractive features. New recruits could not be expected to know much about flying, so there would have to be a good training scheme. This might bring into play the only skill I had to offer the armed services: the ability to study and pass examinations. It also occurred to me that an aircrew was a small unit in which each member might exert some control on his own destiny. Another factor was the influence of the recruitment posters. They had a somewhat civilised look about them, for even the humblest airman wore a collar and tie. Perhaps there would be less unnecessary and irksome discipline.

There was no point in applying to train as a pilot. I had never owned a car or a motor bike and the internal combustion engine was an uninteresting mystery to me. I knew nothing about navigation either, but it might call for the sort of calculations that had appealed to me in the past. Thus, on 9 July 1940, I joined the RAFVR, seeking to become an air observer, which was the title given to the navigator in the recruitment literature.

After three days of examinations, interviews and inoculations, the Board Chairman at Cardington Reception Centre announced my fate. I was to be trained as a pilot! The Chairman seemed to expect an enthusiastic response. Instead, I tried to point out that there had been a mistake. The reaction was short and specific. There were to be no questions and no explanations. I was now in the Royal Air Force.

'Right turn, quick march!'

Once I had been selected for pilot training, everything happened at speed. The first step was to Babbacombe, to be kitted out. From there, we recruits moved a few miles along the coast to No 5 Initial Training Wing at Torquay. We received elementary training in ground subjects, while physical training was high on the list of priorities. We ate well and put on healthy tissue.

From Torquay, our group of trainees were posted to an Elementary Flying Training School at Cambridge, where we began flying in Tiger Moths. The pressure was on and the rejection rate was high. One had to learn quickly or fall by the wayside, sometimes for reasons outside our control. Bad weather restricted the total number of hours available to the course, so that fewer trainees could reach the required number. Although my prowess in ground subjects gave cause for praise, my skill in the air did not develop sufficiently quickly. I was one of the last to be 'scrubbed'. It so happened that the casualty rate among that group of trainees was extremely high during the next two years, so that I can now look back with mixed feelings on that week of bad weather in the middle of October 1940.

So many ex-pupil pilots were queueing up at Babbacombe for training as air observers that a temporary ban was imposed on such remustering, but the Chief Instructor at Cambridge listened sympathetically to my pleas and turned a blind eye to the regulations. Fortunately, no one at Babbacombe raised any objections when I arrived, so that at last the RAF and I were not at odds about how I might best help the war effort.

Suspension from pilot training also brought my first opportunity to apply for leave. Only 48 hours were granted but that was enough for me; I married my wife Hattie on 19 October 1940. The honeymoon had to be delayed for a fortnight, but then Hattie joined me at the hotel in Babbacombe where I was billeted; this was another example of the war effort being helped by the turning of an official blind eye.

There were four stages in the training of air observers: Navigation School, Bombing and Gunnery School, Operation Training Unit, and finally training on an operational squadron. I was one of a group of trainees who were posted to No 6 Air Observer Navigation School at Staverton, near Gloucester, on 9 December 1940. Classroom instruction was provided by former members of the Merchant Navy. They did their best, but to someone accustomed to university and Civil Service standards of instruction, there seemed to be scope for improvement. We were taught rule-of-thumb methods, without much reference to underlying principles. I had an innate objection to doing anything that someone told me was the correct method, without adequate explanation. The long and dark evenings gave me plenty of opportunity for private study to supplement the formal lectures. I delved quite deeply into most aspects of the course, to the amazement and even the disgust of those trainees who preferred the attractions of the canteen. When the course ended on 29 March 1941, I felt that I had acquired a good understanding of the principles of air navigation, as well as associated subjects such as maps and charts, meteorology, signalling and air photography. But I had little confidence in my ability to navigate an aircraft, even in daylight. Our training flights, in Avro Ansons, had usually ended over the required township, but I attributed that accuracy more to the pilot's knowledge of the terrain than to our navigational skill. We had become more accomplished at map-reading than dead-reckoning navigation. Most of my fellow-trainees went to Bomber Command, where proficiency in map-reading must have been particularly important at that stage of the war.

To my dismay, I learnt something else at Staverton. Even before take-off, the smell of an Avro Anson made me feel sick. Soon after we took off, that feeling became a reality, all too often. There was a handle beside the pilot's seat, which we had to wind at great speed to raise or lower the undercarriage. When it was my turn to carry out that chore, the effect on my stomach was usually disastrous. The RAF turned out to have a disadvantage comparable to that of the Royal Navy, with the saving grace that aircraft returned to base after shorter time intervals. It was possible that operational aircraft did not have the same pungent smell; I could only hope for the best.

The next stage of our training was No 10 Bombing and Gunnery School, at Dumfries in Scotland. The Armstrong-Whitworth Whitley Mark IIs, from which we practised air gunnery, were too sedate to upset even my sensitive stomach, but the same could not be said of the Fairey Battles which were used for bomb aiming. I could only claim credit for containing myself until we returned to the runway. I never dropped bombs in an operational squadron and only fired a machine gun on two occasions, so that little need be said about the course itself. An entry in my flying log book records my performance as 'Above average in theoretical knowledge. Requires more air firing practice.' My bomb aiming could have been described as abysmally poor, but some of the other trainees seemed little better.

The conclusion of this course, on 23 May 1941, brought the award of the observer's brevet and promotion, either to the rank of sergeant or commissioning as a pilot officer. There were 30 trainees on the course, nine of whom had been to public school and one, myself, to university. We expected about a third of us to become commissioned officers. In those days, schooling had a very strong bearing on selection. I was delighted to be the first called for interview by the squadron leader responsible for making the recommendations. However, I was very surprised to be greeted with a brusque accusation on entering his room.

'You're not fit to be a navigator!' 'Scandalous.' 'Outrageous.' 'It should be a court martial offence.'

These were just a few of the expressions which punctuated the ensuing tirade. I was too bewildered to guess what misdemeanour I had committed. When in trouble, say nothing. So I waited in silence, hoping for divine intervention.

Eventually, a chance remark from the adjutant, who had been standing behind the squadron leader, revealed the cause of the furore. It transpired that my medical record card, completed in Cardington three days after I had joined the RAF, designated that I was *medically* unfit to be an air observer. The card had been filed away and not re-examined until I was considered for a commission. A lot of effort and expense had been wasted in training me for a job that I was officially unfit to perform.

A lull in the storm enabled me to mention that King's Regulations forbade any airman from knowing the contents of his own medical record, and that up to then I had no knowledge of any medical defect. A heavy silence fell on the room, followed by smiles and sweet reasonableness.

'You've made a good point. . . . it would seem to let you off the hook. . . . unfortunately, it puts someone else right on it. . . . we'll have to do something about it, shan't we?'

We had suddenly been united by a common purpose, and my respect for my commanding officer took a sharp upward turn. It was explained that the fault lay with my eyesight. I had known for a long time that I had an astigmatism in one eye, but presumed that this was so slight as to be of no significance. It was not bad enough to debar me as a pilot but it brought me just below the standard required for an air observer, who needed especially good eyesight to pick out landfalls and bomb targets. At last, my selection for training as a pilot rather than as an air observer could be explained.

The other members of the course were posted to Bomber Command Operational Training Units. I stayed behind, while the wheels of the RAF administration slowly turned. A long series of medical examinations then followed, at increasing levels of authority: bombing and gunnery school, station, group, command, and finally Adastral House in London, where a senior eye specialist held court. Yes, my eyesight was below the required standard, but only just. The standard itself was currently under review and might soon be amended. It would be a pity to waste all that training, at a time when qualified aircrew were so urgently needed. If I was still keen to fly. . . .

The medical officer took out his pen, deleted the letters 'un', and stamped and initialled the amendment. The record then read 'Fit pilot and fit air observer'. He said he hoped I wouldn't mind if he added a rider that it would be as well not to send me on night bomber raids, where a slight defect in the bomb aimer's vision might detract from the effectiveness of the mission. I had no objection whatsoever.

Back I went to Dumfries, to be commissioned and to await posting. That came a fortnight later. It was to No 4 Coastal Command Operational Training Unit, at Invergordon on the Cromarty Firth, in Scotland. It was a base for flying boats which, in those days, many airmen regarded as the aristocrats of the air. This type of operational flying certainly appealed to me as a budding air navigator.

There was a further reason why other trainees might have envied my good fortune. The statistics for aircrew losses (as shown later in a table sent to the Air Member for Personnel on 16 November 1942) showed that aircrew on Catalina flying boats had a 77½ per cent chance of surviving a tour of operational flying. This was the highest survival rate in all types of aircraft. Comparable figures for the other trainees leaving Dumfries were 44 per cent for those posted to heavy bomber squadrons and only 25½ per cent on light bomber squadrons. Needless to say, the figures for two tours were correspondingly far less.

Before leaving Dumfries, on 7 July 1941, I was given a certified copy of Form 657, stating that I was medically classified to serve as both a pilot and an air observer. It was thought that such a certificate might help allay concern if other members of the crew saw me wearing spectacles. It was never necessary for me to produce the form, since only one eye was needed for drift measurements while binoculars could be used quite effectively as a spyglass. However, I have kept the document as a memento of the kindness of fate, for my guardian angel must have been working diligently on my behalf.

I found that I was one of ten air observers posted to Invergordon for operational training. We trained on two types of flying boats, an old Short Singapore and Saunders-Roe Lerwicks. The other nine trainees were Canadians and Australians, whose previous courses had included astro-navigation. A special astro course could not be laid on just for me. I was given the appropriate manual, with instructions to read it up myself and to refer to the others if I needed any help. I required assistance only in the practical use of sextants.

Most of my astro observations were taken from the ground, and I found that I regularly fixed the position of Invergordon to the east or west of its correct longitude. I soon realised that it was my watch which was inadequate. It was essential to have a service wristwatch which recorded Greenwich Mean Time (GMT) precisely; every second of timing error resulted in misplacing Invergordon by one eighth of a mile.

Quite obviously, astro-navigation is only possible when the 'heavenly body' (the sun, moon, planet or star) is not obscured by cloud. In our later Arctic flying, this was rarely the case. Even when the sun was visible, it was usually only for very short intervals. Nevertheless, a good understanding was essential for the tasks that lay ahead. At Invergordon, I had to transpose most of my reading into three-dimensional diagrams to clarify understanding. Perhaps it is sufficient here to say that I took the opportunity to delve much more deeply into the subject than would have been the case on a normal astro course.

After two months at Invergordon, on 9 September 1941, I was posted to 210 Squadron at Oban, on the west coast of Scotland. This was a flying boat squadron which had been equipped with Short Sunderlands since June 1938 but had begun to receive Consolidated Catalinas during April 1941. It was building up to its complement of flying crews while awaiting the arrival of more Catalinas from the USA. Usually, only four aircraft were operational at any one time when I joined the squadron, and these were manned by experienced crews. Thus, there was little opportunity to continue air training during the first weeks. Occasionally, a beginner such as myself could be given the chance to fly as second navigator and watch an experienced man practising his craft.

My mentor at this stage was Pilot Officer George Buckle, a navigator who was approaching the end of his operational tour. We flew on a few transit flights which were uneventful. I learnt how to measure drift accurately over the sea, and developed the art of estimating wind velocity by studying the surface of the water. The stronger the wind, the larger the white caps thrown back from the crests of the waves and the clearer the lane markings made by the wind on the surface of the sea, showing the wind direction. Alert observation of the sea and the sky were basic requirements for good dead-reckoning navigation in low-flying aircraft of Coastal Command.

My last flight as a squadron trainee was on 23 December 1941, under the captaincy of Flight Lieutenant D.C. McKinley, DFC. This was the pilot who later captained the modified Lancaster bomber 'Aries' which flew over the North Pole in May 1945.* My flying log was then endorsed 'qualified for the squadron role'. Three months had gone by since I had joined the squadron, and my contribution to its activities had been very limited indeed.

This was followed, during January 1942, by three short flights as first navigator to Flight Lieutenant C.M. Owen. However, the following month brought a change in our circumstances. The whole squadron, now fully equipped, moved base to Sullom Voe in the Shetlands.

I had expected to make the journey as a passenger with one of the established crews. Instead, I was told the good news that I was to fly as navigator with a captain who had been recently promoted, Flight Lieutenant D.E. 'Tim' Healy. He already had the reputation of a captain to be respected and was fast becoming one of the squadron's personalities. Moreover, he was still looking for a full-time navigator. I had already learned something of his likable character from his second pilot, Pilot Officer Ronald Martin, who praised the compassion with which he had sympathised with the widow of an officer who had lost his life.

The transit flight from Oban to Sullom Voe, on 14 February 1942, was to herald the most eventful period of my service in the RAF. In itself, it was an inauspicious beginning, but it was from such small accidents of fate in war that one's future was sometimes determined. The two men I had the good fortune to join on that day are so prominent in the events of this narrative that more thorough introduction should be made.

Dennis Edward Healy was born on 26 August 1915 in Suez, the second son of Henry Francis and Maud Elizabeth Healy. His father was of Irish parentage and worked for the Eastern Telegraph company, now part of Cable and Wireless, while his mother was a Canadian of Welsh stock. Eventually, another boy and a girl were born in this family.

Henry Healy's job took him and his family overseas and back to England for several periods. In 1916, he worked in the Red Sea area, while his wife and family lived in Southsea. In 1921 the whole family transferred to Capetown, returning to England in 1924. Then he moved to Malta and, after a while, the family joined him there in

* See Epilogue.

Valetta. By now, Dennis was aged eleven and, like his elder brother Brian, was an adventurous and lively boy who was keen on all forms of sport. This was at a period when Britain was still a very strong naval power, and the boys could watch the battle fleet sail in and out of Valetta harbour on manoeuvres. They were also choristers at St Paul's Cathedral in Valetta.

When Henry Healy was appointed to a cable station on the Greek island of Syra, about 80 miles from Athens, a decision had to be taken about the boys' education. They were sent to a small public school at Abingdon, where there was a strong Protestant and classical tradition. Dennis entered into the school activities with great gusto. He rowed, played rugger and hockey, was good at athletics, joined the photographic society, and became a member of the OTC.

In 1931 this education came to a sudden end, when Henry Healy was made redundant. Dennis had matriculated by now, but jobs were hard to find. He worked for a while as a parcel wrapper in the despatch department of Debenhams store, but a better opportunity came when, in 1932, he joined the Gas Light and Coke Company as a staff pupil. There he began his training as a fitter's mate, attending to gas installations from the humblest tenement in London to the splendour of Buckingham Palace. He attended night school and obtained qualifications which led him upwards to the company's secretarial and financial departments. By the outbreak of war, he was an assistant service supervisor in the company's Westminster office, covering an area throughout central London.

In addition to an intense application to his career, Dennis led an active social life. He enjoyed music and dancing, and became a member of a group which performed concerts at charity shows. He also joined the company's amateur dramatic society, where he once took the leading role in a play. This interest in acting led to a meeting with Madeline Rushworth-Lund, a young lady who also enjoyed this activity. They married and went to live in a small bungalow in Stanmore, near his parents. Here their first child, Michael, was born.

Like thousands of other patriotic young men, Dennis was affected by the international tensions and the rumours of war in the late 1930s. He joined the pre-war RAFVR, as a part-time trainee pilot. His initial training was at Fairoaks in Surrey, and he was at the annual camp when war was declared. The next few months were spent at Initial Training Wing at Cambridge, but in April 1940 he was posted to No 20 Service Flying Training School at Cranbourne

(*Top left*) Flight Lieutenant Dennis Edward Healy, DSO.

(*Top right*) Pilot Officer Ernest Schofield, DFC.

(*Bottom right*) Pilot Officer Ronald Martin.

in Southern Rhodesia, to continue his flying training. He was commissioned in November 1940 and moved on to George on the southern coast of South Africa for a course in general reconnaissance, the normal prelude to the entry into Coastal Command.

He arrived back home in the late spring of 1941 for a short reunion with his wife and young son, both of whom he adored, for he had a passionate belief in the happiness of family life. Then followed a posting to the OTU at Invergordon, for conversion to flying boats.

In the summer of 1941, Dennis Healy arrived at Oban to join 210 Squadron, at the time when they were flying with Catalinas. His first flight was on 16 July as second pilot to Flight Lieutenant P.R. Hatfield, a Catalina pilot who, on 26 May 1941, relocated the battleship *Bismarck* after it had eluded the pursuing British warships, thus assisting its interception and destruction. Healy flew regularly with Hatfield for the next four months, engaged primarily on anti-submarine sweeps and convoy escort duties. On one occasion they took a group of special passengers to Archangel in North Russia. They stopped at Invergordon to top up fuel tanks and then had to land at Deer Sound in the Orkneys to remedy an oil fault. They then continued the 17½ hour journey round the North Cape of Norway to Archangel. The passengers continued to Moscow, a personal contact between senior officers of the Allied Forces on the Western and Eastern Fronts. The return journey was nine days later.

I saw little of Dennis Healy during my first few months in the squadron, for he lived outside the officers' mess with his wife Madeline. But I knew of his reputation as both a second pilot and, later, as a captain. He was tall, lithe, and good-looking, with a very alert manner. He normally wore battledress in readiness to be called out to his flying boat, and the badge on his peaked cap was green from salt spray, as befitted a 'boat man'. In the mess itself, his manner was light-hearted and smiling, and he was very popular as well as highly respected. Like all those with the Irish name Healy in the RAF, he was nicknamed 'Tim' and that is how we all knew him.

Tim Healy's breezy and gregarious nature concealed a man of steely resolve, however. He took the business of flying very seriously indeed. In fact he was a perfectionist, preparing for his sorties with extreme care and, so far as humanly possible, leaving nothing to chance. Every tiny item received his attention, to the point where he could be considered over-meticulous. For instance, he always insisted on leaving one blade of each propeller pointing precisely vertically. But no one in his crew objected to his attention to detail. Instead, we tried to live up to it. It was, after all, reassuring for our own safety to fly with such a highly competent captain.

The second pilot, Pilot Officer Ronald Martin, was born in 1918 in South Shields, where his father was a merchant dealing in yeast and other provisions. He attended the local high school and left at the age of sixteen after he had obtained the Cambridge school certificate. Academic studies did not appeal to him; he was far happier on the sports field, playing cricket, rugger, tennis, or taking part in athletics.

His ambition was to join the RAF as a trainee pilot and then to move on to Imperial Airways. Aviation was his main interest, and he studied the theory of flight to the extent of making practical flying models. He was certainly not interested in spending his working life in an office. But parental influence was such that he became articled to an accountant for four years, and entered his father's business in 1938.

Nevertheless, his interest in aviation could not be curbed and he joined the Civil Air Guard Movement. The purpose of this organisation was to train pilots, at the very reasonable rate of five shillings (25p) an hour, and thereby create a reserve of pilots in the event of war. By the end of August 1939, when private flying was brought to a halt, he had managed to complete several hours of flying with the Newcastle Aero Club at Woolsington airfield, now Newcastle Airport.

The 21 age group had registered for national service in June 1939, and Ronald Martin had been earmarked for service in the RAF. His call-up papers arrived in June 1940. The first few weeks were spent in kitting out and drill at Padgate reception centre. From there, he moved to No 5 Initial Training Wing at Torquay, as a pilot under training. By coincidence, I was there at the same time, but we do not remember meeting each other.

Unlike myself, Leading Aircraftman Ronald Martin proved to be a most successful pupil pilot. He was posted to No 6 EFTS at Sywell, near Northampton, where he went solo after only 5½ hours dual instruction. It was normal for trainees to move from EFTS to Service Flying Training School (SFTS), but the need for operational pilots was so acute that a few trainees of above average ability were sent direct to No 13 OTU at Bicester, in Oxfordshire, to convert to twin-engined Bristol Blenheims. However, this experiment proved

disastrous and there were a number of fatal accidents. Ronald
Martin and his surviving colleagues were fed back into the normal
pattern of training.

A short refresher course on Tiger Moths at No 10 EFTS at
Weston-super-Mare was followed by standard twin-engined training, on Airspeed Oxfords at No 14 SFTS at Cranfield in
Bedfordshire. Here he was awarded his wings and commissioned as
a pilot officer.

He had hoped to be posted to a night-fighter OTU but fate and the
authorities decreed otherwise. It is a fact that the steadier pilots of
high ability were destined for long-range work in Coastal Command.
He was posted to No 3 School of General Reconnaissance at Squires
Gate, near Liverpool. Here he flew Blackburn Bothas, considered by
many pilots to be one of the most difficult and dangerous aircraft in
the wartime RAF. However, his performance earned praise and he
passed out in first place in his course. From here, he was posted to No
4 OTU at Invergordon. He converted on to flying boats, first
Saunders-Roe Londons and then Consolidated Catalinas.

His final posting was to 210 Squadron at Oban but, once again, he
required further training, particularly since he had not yet qualified
for night flying on Catalinas. This was completed on the squadron.

During this long period of training, Ronald Martin's interests had
not been wholly confined to flying. In June 1941 he had married his
fiancée, Margaret, whom he had known since shortly after leaving
school. The young couple were able to live for a while outside the
RAF station at Oban. On Christmas Day 1941, Ronald and
Margaret attended a party at the Great Western Hotel. Margaret
noticed a tall, slim and debonair RAF officer leaning against the
piano. He had a glass of beer in his hand and was singing
enthusiastically and tunefully. Impressed by his appearance and
manner, Margaret asked who he was. Her husband proudly
explained that she was admiring his new captain, Tim Healy, and
that they would shortly be flying operationally. Introductions
followed, together with the opportunity to meet Tim's wife,
Madeline.

These were the two pilots whom I was fortunate enough to join on 14
February 1942, on that short transit flight in a Catalina from Oban
to Sullom Voe. The two men addressed each other as 'Tim' and
'Ronnie', and I was known as 'Scho'. The 'Tim-Ronnie-Scho'
relationship started immediately, as the three officers in the crew. It

Flight Lieutenant Healy's crew in February 1942. *Seated left to right*: Pilot Officer R. Martin, Flight Lieutenant D.E. Healy, Pilot Officer E. Schofield. *Standing from left to right*: Sergeant T.R. Thomas, Sergeant H.V. Watson, Aircraftman D. Baird, Sergeant B. Webster, Sergeant G.V. Kingett, Sergeant J.E. Campbell, Sergeant K. Jones.
Seven of these men later flew in Catalina 'P for Peter'.

continued for the next six months of arduous flying, mainly over the Arctic waters to the north of the Shetlands.

We were equally fortunate in the remainder of our crew, all of whom were first-class men. Four of these already knew and respected our captain. These were the wireless operator/gunners Sergeant G.V. Kingett and Sergeant T.R. Thomas, and the flight engineer/gunners Sergeant E.D. Gilbertson and Aircraftman D. Baird. Sergeant J.E. Campbell joined the crew as rigger/gunner, and also proved to be a good cook. The post of third wireless operator/gunner was at first filled by Sergeant H.V. Watson and later by Sergeant J.L. Maffre. In time, Sergeant Gilbertson moved on and was replaced by Sergeant B. Webster, then by Sergeant E.C. Horton, and finally by Sergeant R.M. Smith.

Of all the men in our crew, I had received the longest period of formal education, but there was something which book learning and analytical reasoning had not disclosed to me. This was the way by which the apparently impossible could be achieved by inspired leadership. We were shortly to respond to the personality of the captain of our crew, who brought out in us qualities of co-operation and endurance, together with the will to succeed, which might otherwise have lain dormant. It had a strong effect even on me, and I was unwarlike by nature as well as a somewhat reluctant volunteer. Since then I have often wondered why this force, which can have such an influence in war, is so rarely evident in peacetime. Leadership is difficult to explain and, even when understood, is even more difficult to practise, for it is so closely woven with character and behaviour. In the narrative that follows I shall do my best to describe it.

CHAPTER TWO

Sullom Voe

The locality of Sullom Voe in the Shetlands has now become a bustling terminal for the oil rigs in the North Sea, but the pilots who flew over the RAF camp at the flying boat base in 1942 found little to attract them, unless they took a delight in moorland scenery. Coastal Command specialised in building camps in remote places, but few could have been more bleak than Sullom Voe. The camp itself was similar to many other RAF stations. There were a few administration blocks built of brick, surrounded by Nissen huts and wooden structures, linked by a simple system of inter-connecting roadways. All the buildings were low-lying except a few maintenance sheds and the water tanks on top of the ablution blocks. Camouflage paint covered everything, producing an effect that was even more drab than the surrounding countryside. At nearby Scatsta, there was a short runway which could be used by light communications aircraft. Beyond that, there was nothing but desolate moorland, with not a single tree in sight.

In spite of this environment, we did not dislike our remote base in the Shetlands. Its sheltered tranquillity was always welcome when we returned from a long and tiring flight. As with many other RAF stations, the comradeship and spirit of the squadron compensated for any disadvantages, even though we were an all-male society.

The voice which dominated the lives of all, officers and airmen alike, was the Tannoy loudspeaker. No matter where we were or what we were doing, this great interrupter demanded instant attention. The accent changed with different announcements. It might be Cockney, Scots or Oxford, but when the content was 'the mail is now ready for collection' the intonation did not matter. All messages usually started with 'Attention! Attention!' but when the tone was more cheerful and less authoritarian, we could often guess what was coming, such as an announcement of a film show in the evening. The message which never varied was the twilight greeting every evening: 'Ah-tenshun! Ah-tenshun! Commence station black-aeiout! Commence station black-aeiout!' This was followed a

Catalina flying boat showing pilots' cockpit, floats retracted to form wing tips, the 'step' on the keel of the hull, and the blisters aft of the mainplane. There was a bomb aimer's window in the bows below the front hatch, which is closed in this photograph.

The amphibian PB-Y Catalina. Only eleven of this type were delivered to the RAF, although they were in general use in the US Navy.

few minutes later by the confident assertion: 'Station black-aeiout is now in force!'

The Tannoy also served an important operational function, for it was used to call out the crew of an aircraft when a flight was ordered. It was then the duty of the captain, navigator and first wireless operator to report to the Operations Room for briefing. The second pilot and other members of the crew were instructed to pick up the rations waiting for them at the store. From there, transport would be available to whisk them down to the jetty, so that they could prepare the flying boat for immediate departure. The transport then returned to the Operations Room to pick up the three other men. In addition, pilots and navigators usually visited the operations room and the Intelligence Office daily, to keep themselves informed of the 'daily situation'. The briefing for an urgent flight could thus be quite short. Where a reconnaissance was being arranged for a new development, longer explanations might be needed.

Another use of the Tannoy was for emergency calls. 'Gale crews' were sent on board the flying boats when bad weather approached the base. Maintenance staff were assembled at the slipway when it was necessary to haul an aircraft out of the water for repairs. The great interrupter was an essential part of life on an active service unit. We were in fact a compact and combined working team, with few distractions to divert us from our primary purpose. This was to provide a base from which aircraft could patrol the vast expanses of the North Atlantic and the Arctic Seas, from Norway in the east to Greenland in the west. We were part of Coastal Command, with its headquarters at Northwood in Middlesex. In turn, this was split into various groups, and our Group was No 18, with headquarters staff at Pitreavie Castle in Scotland.

Of course, Coastal Command operated squadrons of both land-planes and flying boats. For convenience and efficiency, there was good reason to prefer landplanes. The capacity to land and take off on water made flying boats specially suitable for a restricted range of activities, but it imposed several disadvantages in terms of cost-effectiveness. Loading a flying boat with fuel, armaments and equipment while it swung and tossed at moorings created difficulties which did not arise on dry land. In order to carry out major repairs and maintenance, it was necessary to haul flying boats out of the water on specially made, detachable chassis; this was an operation which had to be co-ordinated with the movement of the tide twice daily. The exercise was costly in manpower, often requiring teams of airmen to haul on guiding ropes to prevent the aircraft swinging against obstacles as it approached the slipway. There was an amphibian version of the Catalina but it was not used at Sullom Voe, for its range was too short for our type of operations.

The operation of flying boats required both good flying weather and good sea conditions. Gales and rough seas went hand in hand, but it often happened that the sea remained too rough for take-off and landing after the gale had passed by. Thus there were sometimes 'no flying' announcements on days when air conditions seemed perfect. Even when both weather and sea seemed favourable, it might be necessary to cancel an operation because the weather forecast was uncertain. Similarly, aircraft might be diverted to another base or recalled, for the same reason. It is understandable that the RAF used flying boats only for those functions which could not be performed by landplanes.

There is no shortage of inlets around the British Isles, while there are several fresh-water lakes close to the coast. Yet there were surprisingly few settings which could satisfy all the requirements for an RAF flying boat base. This needed a protected anchorage together with a sheltered stretch of water long enough for take-off and landing, whatever the direction of wind and tide. Moreover, the islands and promontories needed to be low-lying so as not to create a hazard, particularly when visibility was poor.

Sullom Voe was well-protected from the full force of weather moving over the North Atlantic, but cloud conditions could deteriorate very quickly. On the north-east coast of the Scottish mainland, Cromarty Firth provided a more sheltered haven, but flying from there added two hours to both the outward and return legs of a northerly patrol. If both Sullom Voe and the Cromarty Firth were closed down, the next alternative landing places were much further south, adding four to six hours of extra flying. Thus there was a need for an adequate safety margin of endurance on all flights. Sometimes our aircraft were scattered, at short notice, to other bases where weather or sea conditions might be more favourable for operations.

There was another limitation of flying boats which had to be taken into account. They were not boats which could fly, but aircraft that could float. An important requirement of sea-going craft is that they are of sufficiently strong construction to withstand the rigours of the ocean. That requirement was not applicable to flying boats. They could withstand the full force of a storm when airborne but they

Twin Vickers .303 K guns, aimed through one of the blister cupolas in the waist of the aircraft. These were later replaced by twin .303s, belt fed.

The twin machine guns in the cupola were replaced by a single .50 Browning in some Catalinas.

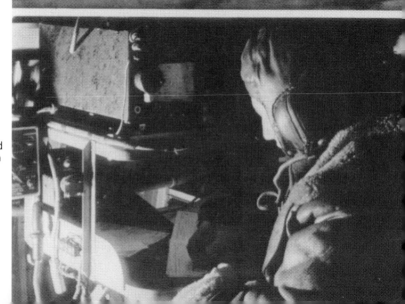

Sergeant T.R. Thomas at the radio desk, which was situated behind the second pilot and on the starboard side of the navigator's desk.

needed protection when water-borne or during take-off and landing. The hulls of our Catalinas were made of duralumin, only 3/32 inch in thickness. Although this was augmented by bulkheads, the construction was fairly fragile. The bulkheads and their watertight doors divided the hull into separate compartments, so that one small hole would not necessarily cause the aircraft to sink when waterborne, but even slight damage could render the aircraft unserviceable.

As regards seaworthiness, the weakest points were the wingup floats. Without their support when waterborne, the slightest roll would have caused the end of the wing to dip into the water, and the 'boat would have capsized. An important characteristic of the Catalina was that the floats were retracted soon after take-off, to form the tips of the high wing, which then had a span of 104 feet. But airworthiness required the floats and their retractable bracing struts to be of light construction. These could withstand the stresses and strains of take-off and landing in sheltered waters, and even those likely to be experienced during rougher weather in protected anchorages. But they could not be expected to ride out severe storms in unprotected waters, nor to withstand bumps or abrasions.

The Catalina normally carried a crew of nine. These were the captain, second pilot, navigator, three wireless operators, two flight engineers and a rigger. The two wireless operators and the flight engineer who were not on duty at their specialist desks manned the machine guns or helped the rigger in the galley. All the crew were qualified air gunners, in addition to their normal tasks.

The pilot's cockpit of the Catalina was quite roomy, with the captain's seat on the port side and the second pilot's seat to starboard, but there was no space for anyone else. Both pilots had a good forward field of vision, but the high wing created blind spots on the rearward quarters, above and behind the aircraft. This source of danger had to be covered by the gunners on watch in the two waist cupolas, or 'blisters'. These egg-shaped perspex domes could be rotated over and inwards, when the .50 Browning machine gun housed in each could be fired. In earlier Catalinas, each blister housed twin .303 inch machine guns, before the larger calibre guns arrived. The blisters were also the normal route for the crew to enter and leave the aircraft, with rigorously-enforced instructions not to swing on the gun mountings. They also gave to the 'Cat' one of its most easily recognisable features.

The pilots' seats were high above the catwalk which ran from the blister compartment right through the aircraft to the front turret, which housed a .303 inch Vickers machine gun on a free mounting. When a crew member passed through the pilots' cockpit to the front turret, his head was level with their waists; he might occasionally climb up the seat supports to look through the windscreen, taking care to avoid the throttle levers. Alternatively he could crawl forward to the front turret, but this was open to the slipstream during flight; it was cold and did not give a very good viewing position. I usually preferred to go aft to the blister compartment, which gave excellent sideways views with a reasonable but limited view forward under the high mainplane.

The manual flying controls for both pilots were linked by a yoke, shaped like an inverted 'U', spanning the cockpit. In the centre was a visual telegraph system, somewhat similar to that on a ship, with lights and switches. This was duplicated in the engineer's compartment, situated in the streamlined 'neck' between the hull and the mainplane. Either pilot could flash the engineer for 'auto rich', 'auto lean', 'floats down' or 'stop engines'.

The Catalina was powered by two 1,200 hp Pratt and Whitney Wasp engines. All the engine-related instruments were in the engineer's compartment, but the engine revolution counters and boost dials were duplicated alongside the pilots' flying panel. There was also a dial which indicated when the two engines were perfectly synchronised. In the centre of the instrument panel, which spanned the width of the cockpit in front of the pilots, there were the controls for 'George', the automatic pilot. This was particularly useful for our long-range work where, on a long leg of 1,200 miles, an error of one degree could build up to a landfall error of 20 miles. Of course, it needed constant adjustment, checking regularly with the magnetic compass, or to counteract changes in the aircraft's trim as the crew moved about their duties. It was usually under the control of the second pilot.

The Catalina carried 1,400 gallons of fuel for a standard operational flight of 18 hours. For longer flights, three additional fuel tanks were installed inside the hull; these increased the supply to 1,800 gallons and extended the length of the standard flight to 24 hours, with a maximum endurance of over 30 hours. The rate of fuel consumption varied with the weight of the aircraft and the type of flying carried out. An airspeed of 100 knots was usually regarded as the optimum for economical cruising, resulting in an average fuel consumption of about 54 gallons per hour on the longer flights;

however, this average covered a wide range, from over 60 gallons per hour at the start of a sortie down to 40 at the end when the aircraft was lighter.

The three extra tanks were placed, one on top of the others, in the bunk compartment immediately behind the door leading to the navigation compartment. To compensate for the extra weight other equipment, such as depth charges, had to be left behind. The presence of these cylindrical tanks called for increased agility from all on board, especially the navigator, who had to move past them more frequently than the others. There was a six inch wide board running along their length, about two feet above the central catwalk. The watertight doors were oval in shape, reaching from knee height to below the shoulders. Even when the tanks were not on the other side, one needed to stoop and twist to get through the opening. It was even worse when carrying a sextant or a plate of food. We needed to be physically fit and agile, particularly towards the end of a long flight.

As the flight progressed, the engineer pumped the fuel from the extra tanks into the main tanks. The internal tanks were usually empty after about six hours flying, and then the stove could be used. First of all, however, the last vestiges of petrol vapour had to be cleared. The procedure for this was simple, if unorthodox. The windows in the pilots' cockpit, the watertight doors separating the internal compartments and the blister cupolas were all opened. A roaring gale of cold and fresh air swept through the aircraft. While this was taking place, the crew kept their noses well covered. We had to go round later, sniffing for any tell-tale whiffs of vapour. Once the captain had given the all-clear, cooking could start and those who wanted to could smoke.

When the Catalina was heavily laden – sometimes overladen – at the beginning of a flight, it tended to wallow somewhat, but this eased off as some of the fuel was consumed. The airspeed then built up, if only by a couple of knots, and it became easier to hold a steady course.

Flying boat crews were seamen as well as airmen. Their craft had to be moored, and they used boat-hooks and anchors. They had to understand tides, and to recognise channels and marker buoys. It was necessary to read the weather, to make forecasts, and to cope with the changes taking place over seas where normal meteorological information was not readily available. As in the remainder of Coastal Command, turns were to port or starboard, not to left or

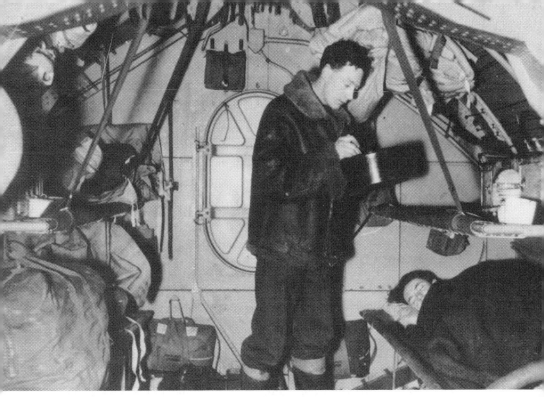

The bunk compartment, aft of the navigator's compartment, in an RAF Catalina. The watertight doors led to the blister compartment. Someone is pretending to be asleep in this photograph, but the bunks were rarely used by the crews in Coastal Command. The cooking was also done in this compartment.

Pilot Officer Ronnie Martin, the second pilot in Flight Lieutenant Dennis Healy's crew, taking a spell at navigating the Catalina. The chair on the left could swing round on an arm, but he is standing on the catwalk between the navigator's desk and the radio desk.

right. Nearly all their flying was close to the sea, usually below 2,000 feet or even just above the waves, dependent on the cloud level, for we needed to maintain visual contact with the sea. Airspeeds were measured in knots and distances in nautical miles. We carried sets of Admiralty charts, and often co-operated closely with the Royal Navy and the Merchant Navy.

The aircraft was not fitted with an astrodome. The navigator stood or sat at a very wide desk, about six feet long, but his astro observations had to be taken through an open blister or through an open window in the pilots' cockpit. There was no heating facility, so that everyone had to rely on extra layers of clothing and hot food to combat the cold, which was sometimes extreme.

Taking off a flying boat required a different technique from that used for a landplane, and it had to be varied to suit the water and weather conditions. Moorings were not slipped until the engines had been started, otherwise the aircraft would have been at the mercy of wind and tide. As the 'boat was taxied to the take-off point, the engines were run at full power for a few seconds to check the ignition and to watch for any drop in revolutions. If all was well, the craft was then turned into wind.

Meanwhile, the crew moved forward as far as possible. The take-off warning was given and the throttles opened fully. The Catalina gathered speed, amid much spray and with a deafening noise. It rose on to the planing section of the hull, at the rear of which was the 'step', a recognisable feature of all flying boats. This step helped to break up the tension of the water, and so permitted the aircraft to rise into the air. Once the 'boat was on the step, the spray moved aft and the pilots had a better forward vision. When fully committed to take-off, a confident pilot could flick the appropriate switch and raise the floats, improving the smoothness of take-off. When the Catalina reached flying speed, a little backward pressure on the control column eased it off the water.

When the water was glassy calm, any flying boat needed a longer run for take-off. The planing bottom tended to stick to the surface of the water and the aircraft might have to be 'pulled off' once flying speed had been reached. The best conditions were when there were little waves or a gentle 'chop', which broke up the surface tension. High waves or a long swell were usually grounds for prohibiting flying. These could throw the 'boat into the air before it had reached flying speed. At best there would be a bumpy take-off and at worst a crash into the next wave, with disastrous consequences. One of the greatest dangers was to allow the 'boat to 'porpoise' while gathering speed on the step, for eventually it would nose-dive under the water, with little chance of survival for all those on board. This tendency had to be checked by easing back slightly on the control column.

The technique for landing a flying boat also had to be adjusted to the state of the water. When the surface was glassy calm, it was difficult to judge height at the end of the approach run. A powered approach over the last 100 feet was considered safest, losing height at a rate of 200 feet per minute until the hull touched the water. The 'boat could then plane on the step for a short distance, giving to onlookers the impression of a gentle kissing action. As the engines were throttled back, the hull settled down into the water amid a cloud of spray. When the surface was well ruffled by the wind, a much steeper approach was made to the last few feet. The pilot then flared out the descent with more power for the touch-down, and then throttled back.

*

In the early months of 1942, several warships of the Kriegsmarine had moved to protected anchorages along the Norwegian coastline. The main threat to Allied shipping in the Atlantic came from the battleship *Tirpitz*, but there were also other units such as the pocket battleships *Admiral Scheer* and *Lützow* and cruiser *Hipper*, together with their attendant destroyers. Against this threat, Coastal Command could deploy only one squadron of torpedo-carrying Beauforts, since the majority of these aircraft had been sent to the Mediterranean to counter an equally serious situation in North Africa as well as the advance of the Japanese towards India. The single squadron was later augmented by two squadrons of torpedo-carrying Hampdens, however. The C-in-C of Coastal Command, Air Chief Marshal Sir Philip Joubert, would have liked to include his long-range flying boats in the strike force, but the Air Staff persistently ruled otherwise. Thus the primary role of our Catalinas remained reconnaissance and convoy protection.

The first of these two tasks became the major preoccupation of the Catalinas of 210 Squadron during their first six months at Sullom Voe. The focus of attention was the Norwegian coastline. Our 'cross-over patrols', shaped like straight-sided figures of eight, were carried out so frequently that they were marked permanently on the wall map in the Operations Room. Each had its own code name. 'Prowl' and 'Prowler' criss-crossed on a north-south axis off the

entrance to Trondheim Fjord, to within five miles of the coastline at
night-times but to within fifty miles during daylight. The 'Brass
Monkey' patrol was further north, along an east-west axis off the
Lofoten Islands.

In the first week of March, intelligence reports indicated that
enemy naval units might be on the move. The resulting 'flap'
brought all serviceable aircraft of our squadron into action. Tim
Healy and the remainder of his crew carried out patrols on 5, 6 and 9
March, of thirteen, fourteen and eighteen hours respectively, but
without any major sightings. On the third of these flights, we saw two
enemy destroyers racing northwards close to the coastline. There
were specific instructions not to leave the patrol line and not to break
W/T silence unless we saw a major unit. Destroyers did not count as
major units, but cruisers and battleships did. If we had searched
ahead of them to find out the reason for the hurry, we might have had
a different story to tell, or perhaps been unable to tell it. This burst of
activity was followed by a fortnight without flying, except for a short
trip on 14 March to enable our squadron commander to give Ronnie
Martin a qualification test as first pilot for day flying. Nevertheless,
we all remained at readiness for the next 'flap' to start.

At night and when there was poor visibility the effectiveness of a
patrol depended largely on the serviceability of our airborne radar
equipment, known as SE (Special Equipment) or ASV (Air to
Surface Vessel). This consisted of a transmitter, which emitted a
narrow beam of radio waves, and a receiver, which could respond to
any waves reflected back by objects in this beam. The receiver
recorded both the outgoing and the reflected pulses and the time
interval between them, converted the time interval into a distance
and displayed this on a scale. The operator looked at a circular dial
with a vertical centre line, about six inches long, marked with a
distance scale. The set could be switched to short or to longer range,
using either forward or beam aerials. An object could be seen on the
screen on the distance scale. If it was not directly in line with the
transmitted beam, it was shown more to one side than the other. A
small object, such as a submarine or a fishing boat, gave a small blip,
while an island or a cliff face produced a larger reflection. A beacon
showed up as a rectangular blob, pulsating to show the identity of the
beacon in morse code.

When we used this radar for searching a stretch of ocean, the
practice was to sweep a band on either side of our track with the
beam aerials. The operator switched over to the homing aerials for a

OPERATIONAL AREA FROM SULLOM VOE

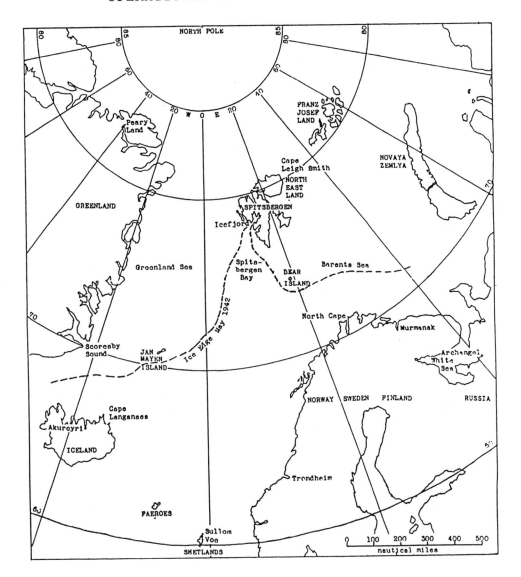

few seconds, at regular intervals, to look ahead. The surface of the water also reflected the radio waves, resulting in a triangle of 'mush' at the bottom of the distance scale. The occasional use of the homing aerials ensured that nothing was lost in that mush. Battleships gave a much more positive reflection than submarines, so that the long-range scale could be used to search for them. One difficulty when searching at night close to the shore was to distinguish land from ship echoes. Even with good equipment, there was need for judgment, and an element of uncertainty.

The weather along the Norwegian coastline could be very blustery. We soon learned that the cold fronts which scudded over the Shetlands could, in due course, cluster alongside the mountains of Norway. On our patrols we could then expect to experience strong winds, low clouds, poor visibility, rain, sleet or snow. It was then essential to have a serviceable radar set. This type of equipment was still in the development stage and, when used for prolonged periods, tended to 'go on the blink'. If this happened at night or in severe frontal conditions, it was foolhardy to continue a low-level patrol close to the invisible coastline. On such occasions, captains had the discretion to alter the patrol line or even to abandon the sortie.

It is understandable that the Admiralty was displeased when unplanned gaps appeared in our squadron's patrol schedules. The Royal Navy had to stay at sea in all weathers, so why should aircraft not remain airborne? It was rumoured that 'moral fibre' was being questioned. This seemed to be confirmed when it was learned that our squadron commander intended to fly with the next sortie, in order to make an independent report on the conditions in the patrol area and the performance of the crew. Wing Commander Hutton was respected by all his aircrews and it was a pleasure to be told that our crew had been selected for this task. Tim Healy's response was typical. He told us that the sortie would have two objectives, to search for enemy naval units and to impress our commanding officer. We took off on 23 March.

The wing commander turned out to be an excellent addition to our crew, going out of his way to gain first-hand experience of all that happened on an operational flight and doing a fair share of the work. He did not carry out any of the specialised jobs, such as work at the flight engineer's desk or at the wireless operator's seat. Nor did he do any of the navigation, but he took a close interest. I thought this was rather too close when he took out his pipe and filled it with evil-smelling tobacco. He was aware of my airsickness problem and that I took pills to counteract it. After a few puffs, he retired to the blister compartment to do a spell of duty on gun watch.

The first few puffs had been too much for me, but work had to go on. Ronnie Martin reported that the wind was freshening and veering, so I stumbled through the pilots' compartment to take a forward drift reading. Many years later, Ronnie told me that Tim and he always knew when something was wrong with me. My shoulders used to bump against their hips when I passed by. When all was well, I used to look up with a grin and say 'Sorry!' On this occasion, there was no such response. Tim nodded to Ronnie, to indicate that he was passing over control, and came down to investigate. Our captain had a simple solution. He returned to his seat and I replaced Ronnie at the controls. Handling the aircraft was a good way to settle a queasy stomach. Five minutes later, I was back at my table working much more happily.

But our commanding officer began to feel less comfortable. The tail of a Catalina could develop a corkscrew-like motion when there was a heavy-handed novice at the controls. After finishing his stint in the draughty blisters, the wing commander returned to the comparative shelter of the navigation compartment, looking cold and not very happy. He was not smoking. It seemed inadvisable to tell him that his discomfort was attributable to my relief.

When we arrived at our patrol area off Trondheim Fjord, a howling gale was throwing back huge 'white horses' from the crests of the waves. As the cloud belt lowered we came down closer to the surface of the sea, increasing the danger from each lurch as the broad wingspan was buffeted by the fierce and eddying air currents. We kept a continuous radar watch as the conditions worsened. We completed several circuits of the patrol and then headed east to the coastline. It seemed a suitable time for our guest to take over another radar watch. The screen was full of vibrating green flashes, mostly reflected by the waves close beneath. The rubber eye-shield banged against his forehead, as the Catalina tossed about. One thing that stood out clearly was the line of mountains straight ahead. I reminded him to give the captain plenty of warning of when to turn away.

It so happened that the radar set chose that moment to misbehave. After turning on to a safe course, Tim came down to investigate and confer. Wing Commander Hutton listened attentively to our discussion, shouted over the roar of the engines. He asked some pertinent questions, to which Tim gave clear replies. In such conditions, even with serviceable radar, it would require a very expert operator to pick up a ship moving close inshore. With an unserviceable set, there was no chance at all. If we continued the patrol, we would endanger the lives of all on board, to no good purpose. If the squadron commander had not been with us, we would have abandoned the patrol. But on this occasion we would stay on patrol until our commanding officer also thought it was time to depart.

The wing commander's response was immediate. 'Call it a day,' he said.

In response to Tim's request for a course home, I took two cards from my pocket, each recording a suitable course from different parts of the patrol, and gave the relevant one to Tim. I then handed the wireless operator a fresh position signal; this was done at intervals throughout our flights, so that he could send a distress signal if an emergency arose. Our guest looked impressed, but made no comment.

Over four hours later, we had left the storm behind and were flying in calm air, but with patches of mist and visibility down to a few hundred yards. Wing Commander Hutton was in the second pilot's seat, while Ronnie was with me in the navigator's compartment. We had been on an unchanged compass course all the way home except for periodic ninety-degree changes to check the wind velocity by the 'two-drift' method. Meanwhile our wireless operator, who was a skilled wireless/electrical mechanic, had managed to make the radar work, albeit intermittently. Ronnie switched it on and used the homing aerials, to hunt for the Sullom Voe beacon. He gave a thumbs-up sign to indicate that it was where it should be, 60 miles away on the starboard bow.

Tim recognised the faint hum over the intercom when the radar was switched on. Normally he would have announced the good news to the crew, so that they could begin their preparations for landing and mooring. But on this occasion he did this by word of mouth instead of over the intercom.

During the next half hour, we made two more turns, ostensibly to check the wind velocity by drift readings. In due course, I stepped through the doorway into the pilots' compartment, nonchalantly eating an apple. Wing Commander Hutton, who was not aware of our success with the radar, leaned down to ask me when we would reach the Shetlands. I looked at my watch and said that the Muckle Flugga lighthouse should appear in front of the starboard wing in a few minutes. He laughed and passed the message to Tim, but dutifully kept watch. Laughter was transformed to amazement when the lighthouse duly appeared through the mist. When he stepped down from the seat, he glanced back at the compass; the course was unchanged.

All the crew treated the perfect landfall as quite normal. The report to the Operations Room was brief: the weather in the patrol area had been atrocious, nothing had been sighted, the radar had become unserviceable, and the patrol had been abandoned. Headquarters must have regarded the flight as unsuccessful, but at Sullom Voe we thought that one of the objectives had been achieved: the squadron commander had been impressed.

During the next morning, Wing Commander Hutton visited the navigation section, where he praised them for the quality of their work and assured them that Group Headquarters were being kept fully informed of the magnificent job they were doing. He was so pleased that he had his photograph taken with the squadron navigators - all except me, for I was in bed. Meanwhile, my log had been analysed in accordance with the usual practice. It was found to be good, but the wing commander had described the navigation as 'unbelievably accurate'. He had unwittingly used the correct adjective. When I described what had happened to the others, they all agreed that the end justified the means. There was no more talk about 'lack of moral fibre'.

That flight, on 23 March 1942, must have been fresh in the mind of Wing Commander Hutton when, a few weeks later, he was asked to select a crew for some special operations. Before that, however, there was an event which aroused our curiosity at Sullom Voe. On 3 April a flurry of interest followed the unexpected arrival of Catalina 'J' of 240 Squadron, from its base at Castle Archdale on Lough Erne in Northern Ireland.

It was our practice to give a warm welcome to aircrews from other squadrons and to exchange information about current activities. On this occasion, however, neither the captain, Flight Lieutenant Desmond E. Hawkins, nor the Canadian navigator, Pilot Officer Jerauld G. Wright, gave any indication for their arrival. Rather mysteriously, they were accompanied by two passengers. These were a Norwegian officer, Captain Einar Sverdrup, and a Royal Navy officer, Lieutenant Alexander R. Glen. These were equally uncommunicative. We noticed that Glen wore a white ribbon, indicating that he was a specialist in the Arctic, while the presence of a Norwegian officer indicated that they might be going to Norway. We could do no more than speculate.

They set off northwards the following day, 4 April. Their flight was recorded in the station Operations Record Book as 'Special flight - secret operation'. Even the members of the sergeants' mess, who were seldom slow to keep abreast of such events, could provide no clues about the nature of their mission. On their return to Sullom Voe, 24 hours later, it became known that the engines had not been switched off. They left the following day with no one being any the wiser as to where they had been.

We know now that their reconnaissance had been authorised on 12 March, the flight being required to take place as soon as possible after 1 April. The objectives were to obtain information about the location of sea ice between Jan Mayen Island and Spitsbergen, to report on the ice conditions in the fjords of West Spitsbergen, and to ascertain whether there were any enemy forces on that island.

The aircrews on our squadron were beginning to regard the Arctic as their own preserve, and they wanted to know why a Catalina from another squadron had been brought in for a secret mission. It was wondered if there was any lack of confidence in the ability of 210 Squadron to carry out such missions. Fortunately, Wing Commander Hutton was able to assure his officers that the next long-range flight from Sullom Voe would be carried out by our squadron. This was confirmed on 11 April by a signal ordering another long-range flight 'to the limit of endurance' to establish the edge of the icefield between Jan Mayen Island and Bear Island, and to find out whether a convoy could pass to the north of the latter.

We in Tim Healy's crew were not aware of this latest development, however, for we had gone on leave on 7 April.

CHAPTER THREE

Spitsbergen

Our first job on returning from leave was to ensure that our Catalina was ready for operational flying. As we came ashore from the air test, the Tannoy was calling for Tim to report to the squadron commander. Ronnie Martin and I returned to the room that we shared, to await any further announcement. But the Tannoy remained silent.

Eventually, Tim came round to see us. He was obviously purring with delight but he took his time in explaining why. When he did open up a little, the quietness of his voice indicated that what he had to say was confidential. He had to take Catalina 'N', serial number AH559, to Gourock on the following day for a major engine overhaul. He had to exchange it for another Catalina, serial W8428, which was being fitted with extra fuel tanks, a DR compass (distant-reading gyro-magnetic), and long-range radar. This aircraft could be used for some long-range reconnaissance flights, each of which was expected to last over 24 hours. While at the Clyde, he would be picking up two passengers who would fly with him as special observers. We were intrigued by his use of the first person singular, for he usually talked about what 'we' had to do, emphasising his belief that successful operational flying depended on team work. The reason for this soon became apparent.

The flights he had been asked to carry out were associated with an operation about which there was such tight security that he could tell us only that all taking part had to be volunteers. He had been authorised to assemble the most competent crew the squadron had to offer. They would have to be tough and self-reliant, and possess sufficient initiative to solve all their problems without normal squadron support. Tim had no wish to make any changes in his existing crew and hoped that they would all volunteer. However, he recognised that the flights would be progressively more hazardous and arduous, and he would fully understand if any members, particularly the married men, preferred not to join him. The crew could expect to be cut off from their families for an unknown length of time and no letters could be exchanged. If anything untoward happened, next-of-kin would eventually be informed by the Air Ministry, in the usual way.

Tim also stressed one other matter, which was of special significance for Ronnie. It was the intention to maintain an unchanged crew throughout the whole series of operational flights. This meant that the second pilot's promotion to captaincy of his own aircraft might have to be delayed. In the meantime, Ronnie would have to regard himself as vice-captain rather than second pilot. Needless to say, both of us promptly volunteered, as did the other members of the crew in due course. We all had such a respect for our captain that if he was prepared to undertake the flights, knowing what was involved, we were happy to go with him.

We were told that there must be no disclosure to anyone about what we were doing, not even to squadron personnel at Sullom Voe. In squadron and station Operations Record Books the description of our activities would be confined to 'Special Flight – Secret Operation'.* Navigation and signals logs would not be handed in to the Operations Room unless specially requested by Headquarters. Many of the normal procedures might have to be bypassed in order to preserve security. We recalled the special operation carried out by Flight Lieutenant Hawkins earlier in the month, but Tim was not to be drawn, except for one clue. He had to ensure that the Catalina he had to collect from Gourock was strong enough to withstand Arctic conditions; if he thought it was unsuitable, he was to reject it and ask for a better one, without disclosing why.

We left Sullom Voe in Catalina 'N' at 11.00 hours on 26 April for the three hour flight to the Clyde. Only one matter was of interest during the flight. This was a long discussion between two members of our crew as to whether the aircraft really needed a major engine overhaul. David Baird, one of our flight engineers, was convinced that the engines were in as good a condition as those of other aircraft in the squadron. But if we were to have a new Catalina, there would be no complaints.

As was usual on such flights, everyone had brought an overnight case, for we never knew how long these detachment duties might last. In the event, we were at Gourock for a week, while the engineers made W8428 fit to fly. While we were away, Coastal Command

---

* Owing to these security measures, the authors needed to search elsewhere to verify the facts about these flights.

Headquarters asked for the names of the selected crew. A cypher message from Sullom Voe gave the answer:

SELECTED CREW COMPRISES F/LT HEALY, P/O MARTIN (PILOTS), P/O SCHOFIELD (NAVIGATOR), SGT KINGETT, SGT THOMAS, SGT MAFFRE (WOP-A/GS), SGT HORTON, A/C BAIRD (FITTERS-A/GS). CREW ALREADY AT GREENOCK COLLECTING CATALINA W8428.

The omission of Sergeant Campbell was an oversight. He accompanied us as rigger/airgunner on all our flights, and proved thoroughly competent. The only changes during the next four months were the promotion of David Baird to sergeant and the replacement of Sergeant Horton by Sergeant Smith. This stable continuity was unusual for a squadron crew and it provided a firm basis from which to develop a very high morale.

Our two passengers soon arrived. Ronnie and I turned up at the slipway to find Tim talking to two officers, a lieutenant-colonel and a lieutenant-commander, both wearing the white ribbon of the Polar Medal. Introductions were made and we were immediately on Christian name terms. They were Lieutenant-Colonel Arthur S.T. Godfrey and Lieutenant-Commander Alexander R. Glen, the former being nicknamed 'Dan' and the latter 'Sandy'. Although everyone at Sullom Voe called me 'Scho', Sandy Glen was one of the few people who addressed me as 'Ernest'.

Dan Godfrey was educated at Eton. After passing out at Woolwich in 1930, he was gazetted to the Royal Engineers. He was a big man, in character as well as build. We soon came to know him as a quiet man, very gentle and reliable. In 1934 he had joined with two others, Martin Lindsay and Andrew Croft, to form the British Trans-Greenland Expedition, the purpose of which was to explore a remote stretch of the East Greenland hinterland between Scoresby Sound and Mount Forel. They completed a strenuous journey, with sledges and dog teams, across the Greenland icecap from west to east, in the region of latitude 70 degrees North. It involved climbing to over 10,000 feet, taking all their food and equipment with them.

Sandy Glen went to Kelvinside Academy and Fettes before moving on to Balliol College, Oxford, where he read Geography. His Arctic experience was gained mainly in Spitsbergen, or the Svalbard Archipelago as it is more accurately named by the Norwegians. He explored in northern Spitsbergen in 1933/4 and again for a longer period in 1935/6, when he was the leader of an expedition to North

East Land; the successful completion of this work earned for him the Patron's Medal of the Royal Geographical Society. He was shorter than Dan Godfrey, lightly built, very enthusiastic and loquacious. He had a number of unorthodox jobs as a young lieutenant in the RNVR, before being appointed to 'HMS President', headquarters of the London Division RNVR, for special duties with the Director of Naval Intelligence. He had obviously been appointed to contribute his specialised experience of Spitsbergen. But Dan Godfrey's participation was entirely coincidental. Glen has recalled in his autobiography their chance meeting outside Boodles in St James's Street.

'Are you going anywhere?' asked Dan.

'Yes,' said Sandy. 'Spitsbergen.'

'Can I join?'

'Certainly,' replied Sandy, and the deal was done.

These were the two 'passengers' who were to fly with us, although we did not know all these details about them at the time. Similarly, we knew little of the territory that was to become the focus of much of our attention during the next few months. Apart from Tim, none of us yet knew the reason for our appointment for special flights, which must now be explained.

*

Allied sea convoys to North Russia could be attacked by surface raiders, by U-boats, and by the Luftwaffe operating from bases in northern Norway. It was essential to route the convoys as far away as possible from the Norwegian coastline. To do this, the Admiralty needed to know the rate at which the southern edge of the Arctic icepack could be expected to recede northwards during spring and early summer. This information was required for the whole of the Arctic seas from Greenland, Iceland and Jan Mayen Island in the west, to Spitsbergen, Bear Island and Novaya Zemlya in the east. It was especially important to know the position of the ice between the North Cape of Norway and the South Cape of Spitsbergen. These headlands are 350 miles apart, and between them is the rocky outcrop of Bear Island. Only 120 miles of sea separates Bear Island and Spitsbergen. This is obstructed by heavy drifting ice during most of the winter and spring, but it becomes more open in May. It was imperative that the Admiralty knew the prospects for clear sea-room as far north as possible, particularly since the 24 hours of daylight between late April and early autumn added yet another advantage to the attacker.

The Arctic icepack is not stationary, but undergoes a general circular movement. One of the oceanic currents flows from the region of the New Siberian Islands towards the North Pole, eventually seeking an outlet into the Greenland Sea to the west of Spitsbergen. This movement is so regular that it is known as the Transpolar Drift. In 1937/8 a Russian expedition plotted its path while drifting with the ice from near the North Pole towards North East Greenland, over a period of eight months. However, the state of the ice varies from year to year and from week to week, so that forecasting its movements requires regular examination.

The flight made by Flight Lieutenant Hawkins of 240 Squadron, from Sullom Voe on 4/5 April, had established that the ice around Spitsbergen and in the Barents Sea was exceptionally severe, while that in the Denmark Strait, between Iceland and Greenland, was known to be unusually light. Senior officers of the Royal Norwegian Navy wondered if there might have been a repetition of the conditions last experienced in 1919. Then, the main outflow of ice from the Arctic Ocean was believed to have been diverted from its usual path into the Greenland Sea and to have entered the Barents Sea instead, through the two channels between Spitsbergen, Franz Josef Land and Novaya Zemlya. This possibility did not bode well for the forthcoming Russian convoys. The Norwegians recommended that aerial reconnaissance be carried out to examine these three possible outflow channels. After taking into account daily wind and temperature changes, it would then be possible to forecast the ice conditions that would affect the convoys at the critical parts of their passage throughout 1942. Further benefits would also accrue if weather stations could be set up in Spitsbergen and on Bear Island.

Tim Healy was the captain chosen for these flights. The specialised knowledge of the various types of ice formation would be provided by the two Arctic explorers, Sandy Glen and Dan Godfrey. The Norwegians suggested that some of the flights could start from Advent Bay in West Spitsbergen. It was expected that ice conditions in that region would improve sufficiently to permit setting up an advanced base for a Catalina by the end of May.

These proposed reconnaissance flights, comprehensive in themselves, formed only part of more ambitious plans currently being made by the Allied Command. The flights, the first of which was

SPITSBERGEN

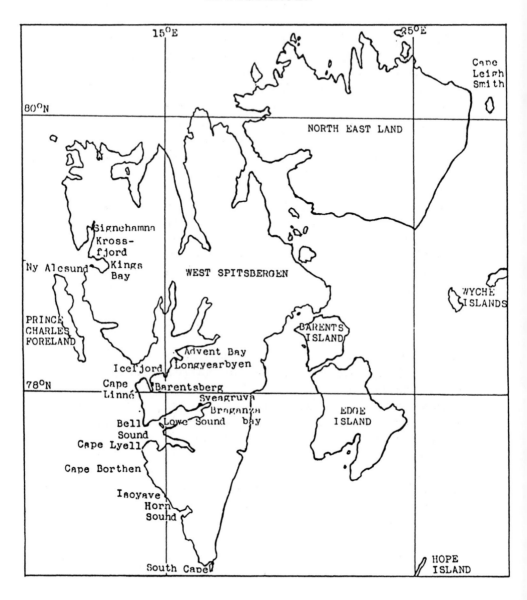

soon to become urgent, were to be integrated with a Norwegian expedition to Spitsbergen.

The archipelago of Spitsbergen is little known to the rest of the world, although its geographical position is of increasing significance. Its borders were recognised by an international treaty drawn up in 1920, the territory being defined as: '. . . comprising, with Bear Island, all the islands situated between 10 degrees and 36 degrees East of Greenwich and between 74 and 81 degrees latitude North, especially West Spitsbergen, North-East Land, Barents Island, Edge Island, Wiche Islands, Hope Island, and Prince Charles Foreland, together with all islands great or small and rocks appertaining thereto.'

Apart from Bear Island, the Svalbard Archipelago, as it is known to the Norwegians, lies to the north of the 76th line of latitude, about 350 miles further north than the North Cape of Norway. It is a rugged, desolate and mountainous area, with a few narrow stretches of coastal plain and some alluvial river beds in steep-sided valleys. The mountains are mostly white-capped throughout the year. Some have glaciers tumbling down to the sea. In winter the whole territory is covered by snow, while the sea adjacent to the shoreline is frozen into a broad expanse of bay ice.

The western coastline of West Spitsbergen is gashed by fjords. The largest, Icefjord, is over ten miles wide in some places. These fjords enjoy the warming influence of the Gulf Stream, however, so that the sea is free of ice in the summer months. A few townships developed in this area, such as Longyearbyen and Barentsberg in valleys running southwards from Icefjord, Ny Alesund in Kings Bay further to the north, and Sveagruva in Van Mijen Fjord to the south. Since the archipelago was so remote and communications within it were so difficult, the settlements developed independently of each other, each attracting different nationals. The international treaty recognised the overall sovereignty of Norway but it acknowledged the rights of settlers from other contracting parties, particularly with regard to mineral and fishing rights. Moreover, Norway undertook not to construct any fortifications or to allow the establishment of any naval base.

Between the two world wars, the population of Spitsbergen was less than 3,000. These were mostly Norwegians and Russians, for although there was no government in Russia at the time the treaty was drawn up, the rights of the settlers were respected. Most of the inhabitants were engaged directly or indirectly in the coal mining activities which had given rise to the settlements. The mine shafts ran straight into the sides of the fjords, and the coal was transported by overhead cableways or along railway tracks to the shoreline. It was stacked during winter, to await the summer thaw. By the outbreak of war, Spitsbergen was producing over 500,000 tons of coal per year, just over half going to Norway and the rest to Russia. The main Norwegian mines were at Longyearbyen in Advent Bay off Icefjord and at Sveagruva to the east of Bell Sound. Those operated by the Russians were at Barentsberg in Green Harbour, a fjord off Icefjord, and at Grumantbyen and Pyramiden further to the east along Icefjord. These unfamiliar names were to become part of our lives in Tim Healy's crew during the late spring and summer of 1942.

In May 1940 the German forces completed their occupation of Norway but did not continue to Spitsbergen. They had more to gain from normal trading relations than from mounting an operation. Life in Spitsbergen continued much as before, apart from the exodus of a few loyal Norwegians who sailed in coal ships to Allied ports. Meteorological reports continued to be broadcast. When a fire broke out in a coal mine at Longyearbyen in April 1941, the Germans dropped fire-fighting equipment from an He111 of the weather reconnaissance unit at Vaernes, near Trondheim. On the following day, Feldwebel Rudolf Schütze landed on an airstrip at Advent Bay, carrying heavier oxygen equipment. The Germans were to benefit later from this experience.

The situation changed after the German invasion of Russia in June 1941. Britain was already concerned about coal shipments to Norway, and it seemed probable that the Russian miners at Barentsberg might now be at risk, together with their coal supplies. The Allies agreed to render the coal mines inoperable under Operation Gauntlet. The cruisers *Nigeria* and *Aurora* sailed from Scapa Flow in August 1941, together with escorting destroyers. They were accompanied by the liner *Empress of Canada* and about 650 troops, mostly Canadians but with some Norwegians and a few British sappers. Two of the British officers were Lieutenant-Colonel A.S.T. Godfrey and Lieutenant A.R. Glen.

The expedition removed or destroyed vital equipment at the coal mines. The coal dumps were set on fire. All the miners and settlers were rounded up and embarked, apart from one Norwegian conscientious objector who went into hiding. Wireless transmissions continued on normal lines, except that weather reports were falsified to discourage the Luftwaffe from sending out reconnaissance aircraft. One man who objected strongly to the destruction was Einar Sverdrup, a determined and tough director of the Store Norske Spitsbergen Kulkompani Aktieselskap, the Norwegian coal mining company at Longyearbyen. This remarkable man was descended from Otto Sverdrup, the captain of Nansen's *Fram*; one of his brothers was a leading oceanographer, while another was a major-general in the US Army. Einar Sverdrup insisted that only key installations such as the power stations and ropeways should be destroyed. He also recommended leaving behind a small and mobile striking force to prevent the establishment of an enemy foothold in the territory. Glen and Godfrey agreed with him, but the Canadian commander could not concur, for he had his orders to carry out. The expedition completed its work and sailed for Britain on 3 September 1941, arriving without loss.

After the evacuation, the Germans and the Allies used reconnaissance and intelligence to discover what the other side was doing. Contrary to Allied expectations, the Germans did not attempt to use Spitsbergen as a base for attacking Russian-bound convoys. They considered that the facilities in Norway were adequate for this purpose. Their main interest was in gathering meteorological information, for this was needed for their military operations in Europe, whether on land, at sea or in the air. The Arctic is the source of many of the cyclonic weather conditions which sweep over north-west Europe. But by August 1941, the Allies had been able to deny to the Germans weather reports from Greenland, Jan Mayen Island, Spitsbergen and Bear Island.

The response of the Germans was swift and comprehensive. Of course, U-boats transmitted weather reports, while other data were collected by the flights made by weather reconnaissance aircraft. Trawlers and sealers were used for a time, but these were vulnerable to attack. The German solution was to set up weather stations, both manned and automatic. In a vast undertaking, sites on land were explored, to which meteorologists and supplies could be transported.

The Kriegsmarine and the Luftwaffe seemed to operate independently of each other. When automatic equipment was sent by U-boats, the containers were tubular so that they could be handled in the same way as torpedoes. In other instances, small parties of meteorologists and their equipment were transported by surface vessels. Such a unit was set up in northern Spitsbergen in the autumn of 1941, at Lilliehöökfjord, a northern arm of Krossfjord. From there, a six-man team supplied the German high command with regular weather reports until they were evacuated by U-boat in August 1942.

A further flow of information was provided by Wettererkundungsstaffel 5, a meteorological unit of the Luftwaffe's Luftflotte 5 in Norway. It was based at first at Vaernes, near Trondheim, but then moved up to Banak, close to North Cape of Norway. From there, He111s and Ju88s carried out flights over Spitsbergen and the Greenland Sea towards Jan Mayen Island and Greenland. The Arctic experience gained by these airmen enabled them to begin setting up and servicing both manned and automatic weather stations in the far north. It was the airmen from Banak who first investigated the reason for the cessation of the coal shipments and wireless transmissions from Spitsbergen, after the Allied expedition in the late summer of 1941. They soon saw the burning coal dumps and the destroyed installations. The settlements were deserted, apart from one man who waved to them.

The Germans considered that a manned weather station should be set up near Icefjord, but there was little time before the onset of the winter freeze and darkness. The most suitable site was near Advent Bay. The broad expanse of a valley provided a clear approach run for aircraft, there was accommodation and other facilities at the nearby township of Longyearbyen, while a subsoil of fine alluvial gravel formed a good base for a landing strip. Moreover, the south-easterly lie of the hills did not interfere with wireless communication with Banak.

Many of the decisions regarding the weather station were taken by Dr Erich Etienne, a man whose Arctic experience dated back to 1936 when he was a member of an Oxford University expedition to West Greenland. The airstrip was marked out in a north-west to south-east direction, about 1,800 yards long and 250 yards wide. It required little surface clearing. The ground was firm when dry and firmer still when frozen, but likely to become boggy after heavy rain or during the spring thaw. The nearby Hans Lund Hut was used as a control and signalling station, with an auxiliary radio station at the Inner Hjorthamn Hut further to the south-east. The site was given the code-name 'Bansö', derived from a combination of Banak and Spitsbergen Öya.

German aircraft began to ferry personnel, equipment and stores to Bansö on 25 September 1941. But their activities were soon detected by the British, using Enigma equipment at Bletchley Park, for the Germans were much more lax about radio communication than the

A Heinkel 111 and a Junkers 52 being loaded with equipment for the German weather station 'Bansö' at Longyearbyen in Spitsbergen, in 1941.

A Heinkel 111 at Longyearbyen in Spitsbergen, in 1941.

Arctic Airmen

Longyea.byen and Advent Bay photographed from a Heinkel 111 in the early summer of 1942.

The station hut of 'Bansö' near Longyearbyen.

Allies; their communications with Banak were detected and decrypted. Four minesweepers, returning to Britain from Archangel, were ordered to investigate. Two of them entered Icefjord on 19 October and headed towards Advent Bay, but they were spotted by a German reconnaissance aircraft from Banak. Within minutes, this reconnaissance aircraft and two Ju52s had taken off from Bansö, carrying 30 men back to Banak. The British party found the site deserted, but the Germans had left in such a hurry that they had even left some code-books behind.

As soon as the minesweepers departed, the Germans moved back again. By 9 November, after 38 sorties had been flown, a four-man team under the leadership of a physician, Dr Albrecht Moll, was operating the weather station. This team continued to supply the German high command with data throughout the winter of 1941/2, as did the station at Lilliehöökfjord further north. Needless to say, some of this information was intercepted and decrypted by British Intelligence.

By early 1942, Spitsbergen assumed renewed importance in the planning at the British Admiralty. Influential Norwegians in Britain had made representations, asking for the prevention of further deterioration of the coal mines. They contended that there would be urgent humanitarian and economic needs for the coal in Northern Europe when hostilities were over. But naval and other officers did not consider this matter was a priority. To them, strategic considerations were paramount. The German advances into Russia had created an urgent need for military supplies to be shipped to Archangel and Murmansk, and Spitsbergen had acquired a new significance for the Arctic convoy route. The sheltered waters of the fjords might provide bases for refuelling escort vessels, while there was a need to prevent the Germans from using landing strips in the territory as bases for attacking the convoys. Some sort of Allied occupation seemed to be required.

At this stage of the war, Britain's over-stretched resources did not permit a large-scale operation to such a distant territory, but the Norwegians contended that only a small force would be required. The men should possess a detailed knowledge of the terrain and be accustomed to living in Arctic conditions. The Norwegians could supply an ice-breaker and a sealer which had taken refuge in Britain, as well as sufficient dedicated stalwarts for the enterprise. These men would need only basic military training. In effect, they would not be an invading force, but a group of patriots returning to their homeland. To that extent, the terms of the treaty would be respected, while the use of Spitsbergen by the enemy would be denied. Eventually, the proposed operation had to satisfy both the strategic objectives of the Admiralty and the civil objectives of the Norwegians.

When Flight Lieutenant Desmond Hawkins made his flight on 4/5 April, the crew and the accompanying observers, Sandy Glen and Einar Sverdrup, were greeted by brilliant sunshine over Icefjord. They saw the coal dumps still burning at Grumantbyen and Barentsberg, but saw no signs of smoke over Longyearbyen. They were delighted to note that the whiteness of the snow was unmarked by man. Unfortunately, they did not penetrate Advent Valley as far as Bansö. Had they done so, they could not have failed to notice the German meteorologists. On their return, they reported that they had seen no one in any of the settlements over which they had passed. The possibility of a successful landing by the expedition seemed to have been confirmed.

The proposed expedition was given the code-name of Operation Fritham. The first contingent of about 85 men was to sail from the Clyde in the ice-breaker *Isbjørn* and the sealer *Selis*, for Akureyri on the north coast of Iceland. After taking on further supplies, the two vessels would head for Spitsbergen. Three British officers would accompany the expedition. They were Lieutenant-Colonel A.S.T. Godfrey, Lieutenant-Commander A.R. Glen and Major A.B. Whatman of the Royal Corps of Signals.

The reconnaissance flights that Tim Healy and his crew were ordered to undertake were associated with this expedition. There was yet another objective for the flights, which will be related in the next chapter. Our precise orders were detailed in a memorandum dated 24 April 1942, sent from the Headquarters of Coastal Command to the Air Officer Commanding 18 Group.* As yet, Tim Healy was the only member of the crew who knew all the contents.

*

The delay in the preparation of our Catalina had to be accepted, but neither of our passengers liked to waste time. It gave them an opportunity to explain some of the purposes of our next flights and to describe ice reconnaissance. Sandy Glen proved to be an excellent mentor. He produced an Admiralty chart of the Greenland and

* See Appendix I

Barents Sea and drew lines all over it to show how the ice pack moved slowly northwards during the spring and early summer. He explained that the speed at which it receded varied year by year, and the Admiralty would like to have reports of its position at intervals over the next two months. At the ice edge, the mixture of warm moist air and cold air usually gave rise to fog, often developing into freezing fog, but he seemed sublimely confident of our ability to overcome this hazard. He then showed us a simple code that had been devised to distinguish five different types of ice:

A. *Pack Ice*. Sometimes known as 'field ice', this was present over the whole of the Arctic Ocean. It was likely to be fractured by the underlying currents and at its edges it was often split into 'leads' of open water. Ice movements could open and close these leads very rapidly.

B. *Drift Ice*. Sometimes known as 'sea ice', this was the first stage in the splitting up of pack ice into separate floes.

C. *Brash Ice*. This was greyish water-logged ice in the final stage of melting.

D. *Bay Ice*. This was solid ice clinging to the shoreline in bays and fjords, where sea currents and winds had less influence.

E. *Icebergs*. These were huge masses of ice which sometimes tumbled from glaciers along the coast of Greenland and, to a lesser extent, of Spitsbergen. They formed a hazard to shipping as they floated southwards.

In addition to reporting the type of ice, estimates had to be made of the proportion of sea covered by it. This was to be done in tenths, as with the proportion of sky covered by cloud. Another requirement was the size of the floes, to be recorded by a numerical code:

1. Up to 20 feet
2. 20 to 200 feet
3. 200 to 600 feet
4. 600 to 1 mile
5. Over 1 mile

These assessments were to be supported by photographs taken simultaneously, if possible. My function was to plot the track of the aircraft, while Sandy would move from the navigation compartment

Ice Edge 75.11 North 18.00 East on 14 June 1942.

Drift ice covering 9/10th of sea. 75.40 North 17.40 East on 14 June 1942.

to the blister compartment and back again, recording the ice conditions on the chart.

While Sandy and Dan continued to give me the benefit of their experience, Tim and Ronnie and the other members of the crew watched with increasing impatience the progress with the aircraft. Finally, it was ready for an air test on 2 May. Only a scratch crew was necessary for the test, and the rest of us gathered on the slipway, surrounded by all our gear in readiness for a rapid departure for Sullom Voe. We were scheduled to fly operationally to the Arctic on the following day.

We had developed a dislike for Catalina W8428. It was obviously an old and reconditioned aircraft that had already logged a lot of flying hours. Tim was under orders not to be fobbed off with a second-rate Catalina, and we were hoping that something would go wrong. Tim brought the flying boat down perfectly, with a clean line of white foam cleaved by the hull. But then the klaxon blared an emergency warning. Some rivets in the hull had been sprung and water was spurting into a midships compartment.

This was the last straw for Tim. A flying boat that behaved like that in the Clyde would be useless in the Arctic. He rejected W8428, and the officer in charge of the maintenance base could not provide a better one. Tim immediately instructed us to put all the equipment back into AH559 and we took off without delay. On returning to Sullom Voe, we reported that our trip to Gourock had been a fiasco. But at least we knew that our first long-range flight to the Arctic would be in an aircraft in which we had confidence. In addition, Tim had learned more at Gourock from Sandy about Operation Fritham than Wing Commander Hutton had learned at Sullom Voe. Ronnie and I were as yet unaware of this expedition. We knew only that the flight was to be an ice reconnaissance and that the passengers were to be put ashore at Spitsbergen.

We arrived back at Sullom Voe at 18.15 hours on 2 May. The ground crew had to work quickly to fit up our aircraft for the following day, but they responded with skill and zest. After a night's sleep, each crew member spent the morning fully occupied with his own sphere of activity. Briefing took place after lunch.

Sandy and Dan accompanied Tim, Sergeant Kingett and myself to the Operations Room. Our briefing did not follow the usual pattern. There was a telephone conversation between Wing Commander Hutton and the Senior Air Staff Officer at No 18 Group, following which we learnt that intercepted radio signals indicated that there was an enemy presence at Spitsbergen. We were asked to make an examination of the old radio station at Quade Hock in Kings Bay, if possible. Tim was given the authority to land at Spitsbergen, at his discretion; he was the officer in charge, not Dan or Sandy. Sergeant Kingett was issued with special coils and crystals for different stages of the flight; he was to maintain W/T silence throughout the flight, except in an emergency, when distress calls could be sent on both high and medium frequencies. The weather forecast was for light winds and absence of storms, with the probability of fog at Spitsbergen and along the ice edge. Sandy chatted with enthusiasm and good humour, while Dan was quiet but observant. When we were ready to go, I took an air-sickness pill.

On the way to the slipway, our transport stopped at the carpenter's workshop. Dan jumped out and returned a couple of minutes later with a bundle of wood, a packet of screws, a screwdriver, and a brace and bit. No one asked any questions. He was the sort of man in whom one placed an instinctive reliance.

The other crew members had ensured that everything was ready on board. All extra equipment, including our overnight cases, had been weighed and stored. Dan's collapsible dinghy was stowed in the tail compartment. Everyone assembled in the navigator's compartment, or around the doors, for the captain's briefing. I opened the Admiralty chart of the Greenland and Barents Seas, and spread it over the table.

Tim explained that our flight had three objectives, all of which were classified as 'most secret'. There must be no mention of them at Sullom Voe, Iceland, or elsewhere. The first purpose was to carry out an ice reconnaissance from Bear Island to Spitsbergen, with the aid of our two passengers, coupled with photographs. The next objective was to carry out a reconnaissance of Spitsbergen, particularly around Icefjord, looking for signs of human activity which must be assumed to be German. The third purpose was to look for some sheltered water close to the shore at Icefjord, sufficiently clear of floating ice to attempt a landing. If we found a suitable anchorage, one crew member would paddle the passengers ashore in the dinghy, where the two men would remain in preparation for another operation. While this was taking place, the rest of the crew would be on full alert and take off at the first sign of danger. If this occurred, the crew member in the dinghy would have to take refuge in Spitsbergen until he could be picked up later. In any case, the aircraft would continue to Jan Mayen Island and Iceland, where we would land after having completed the further ice reconnaissance. There would be W/T silence throughout, but signals would be transmitted to us at six-hourly intervals and decoded on the Syko machine*. The flight was expected to last for 24 hours, so that fuel consumption would have to be carefully monitored, and we would probably be away from base for seven days.

Engines were started at 14.20 hours, but we had to return to the mooring buoy to repair a defect in the automatic pilot. We were eventually airborne at 15.11 hours and flew visually to Muckle Flugga lighthouse, the most northerly point of the Shetlands, from where we set course at 15.32 hours. The pilots noticed a discrepancy of ten degrees between the distant-reading compass† and the magnetic compasses in their cockpit. By checking with the astro compass, it was found that the distant-reading compass was in error, probably as a result of an electrical fault. Temperature was above zero, but there were mist and fog patches. We headed into a light northerly wind, at a height of 1,500 feet, and it was possible to take a few sun sights with the marine sextant.

At 18.46 hours, we came down to 350 feet to pass under a frontal belt of cloud, and then had to skirt round low patches of cloud for the next three hours. Winds remained light and visibility poor.

After about six hours' flying we had used up all the fuel in the internal tanks and were able to remove all traces of vapour by sending a cold blast of air through the aircraft, following which we were able to use the stove and enjoy a hot meal. On one of my drift-taking excursions to the bunk department, I was surprised to see Dan drilling holes through two of his skis. When I next returned on this periodic exercise, the skis had wooden slats attached to them and he was experimenting with ways of fastening his rucksack to a most effective sledge. On my next trip, the device had been dismantled and the wooden slats were back in a bundle, with the tools and screws tucked away in his battledress. Self-reliance was obviously one of Dan's many qualities.

*A simple but effective encrypting and decrypting device carried by many RAF aircrew. The code changed every 24 hours, in the form of a card which slotted into the device.
†The master unit of this gyro-magnetic compass was positioned in the tail, where it was less affected by the magnetism of the aircraft itself.

At 22.30 hours, a strident blare on the klaxon brought us all to action stations and duties. An aircraft had been sighted on the western horizon, but it disappeared into cloud before the blister gunner could recognise whether it was a Catalina or a Dornier. Tim turned to investigate, but resumed course after three minutes, and the aircraft was seen no more. I was too busy working out our position and handing it to the wireless operator to see anything.

By midnight, we were flying at 700 feet, with a temperature of minus two degrees Centigrade. The wind was veering and increasing in strength. As the temperature dropped more rapidly, rain showers were replaced by snow squalls. The first sighting of brash ice came at 01.40 hours, and this was soon followed by drift ice. Sandy and Dan kept a running record of the ice conditions, while I took photographs with the heavy hand-held F24 camera, cranking the sturdy handle. This was the standard RAF camera, with a fixed speed and aperture, but the narrow slit had been widened to cope with fog and Arctic twilight.

The temperature dropped to minus twelve degrees Centigrade. Soon after we passed over the first edge of the drift ice, the homing aerials of our radar showed Bear Island on the starboard bow, and we altered course towards it. We had been flying for over ten hours.

When four miles away from Bear Island, we set course for South Cape of Spitsbergen. The temperature was down to minus 16 degrees and the cloud base down to 500 feet. Visibility was poor, but we were still able to continue with the ice reconnaissance.

As we approached Spitsbergen, the fog thickened and the temperature dropped to minus 19 degrees. A permanent watch was kept on the radar screen as we homed on South Cape. At 03.20 hours Ronnie glimpsed the towering cliffs, before Tim turned away for safety. We crawled along the western coastline for three quarters of an hour, mainly by radar, and only occasionally saw land. Then the fog became so thick that we could barely see our wingtips. It was obviously impossible to reconnoitre the territory in such conditions, and we had no option but to turn away in the direction of Jan Mayen Island.

The cloud base lifted as we moved away from Spitsbergen and the temperature rose by eight degrees. We were traversing the ice-free waters of Spitsbergen Bay, warmed by the Gulf Stream. It was possible to relax a little and to eat a hot meal.

By 05.35 hours drift ice appeared again, with its attendant fog. We dropped down to 100 feet and were forced to alter course continually

Two views of the abandoned Norwegian settlement of Longyearbyen in Spitsbergen. The top photograph was taken by the crew of Catalina J of 240 Squadron, captained by Flight Lieutenant D.E. Hawkins, in April 1942. Undetected at the time, a German meteorological party was established 4 km to the south-east.

to avoid fog patches down to sea level. There were wide stretches of pack ice beneath us, so that Sandy and Dan were busy at work, plotting and recording, and asking for photographs.

On these long-range flights, it was usually at this stage that the feeling of isolation was at its most intense. We were a long way from home. It had been very cold for a long time. We were all getting tired. The pilots had been under continuous strain for hours, as the aircraft skimmed over drift or pack ice. Ronnie Martin can recollect his impressions of flying on this day:

> In order to be as helpful as possible to Scho, Tim and I tried to steer a steady course and speed. This was in the knowledge that a two-degree compass error on a leg of 1,200 miles, without any landfalls or radio bearings or sun sights owing to cloud, would produce an error of 40 nautical miles. Scho would not have been happy with that, to say the least.
>
> The aircraft felt very unstable for the first few hours of every long flight. Later on, when we were overloaded with supplies for Spitsbergen, it wallowed rather than flew until we had used up about 400 gallons of fuel.
>
> Although 'George', the automatic pilot, did most of the straight-and-level flying, its gyros which kept the controls steady were subject to precession, or wandering. Thus we had to check constantly with the various compasses and make numerous small adjustments. As some of the crew walked fore and aft in the fuselage, the aircraft dived or climbed slightly, so that we had to adjust for these movements. Then the trim of the aircraft altered as the fuel was used, so that now and again I disengaged George, adjusted the elevator control, and re-engaged it.
>
> On this day, it was very disappointing to find Spitsbergen shrouded with fog. Sandy sat in my seat for a while hoping to get a glimpse of the land, but we were unlucky. After we turned towards Iceland, Tim left his seat to confer with Scho. I rested my heels on the rudder pedals so that whenever George adjusted the rudder I could feel the movement. This helped to keep me awake.
>
> Flying over the ice at about 100 feet was very tiring on the eyes, although we wore yellow visors to reduce the white glare. Also the steady drone of the engines had a soporific effect, especially during the last quarter of a long flight. Although this flight was shorter than some that followed, merely 23 hours, I found it was the most tiring, possibly because the circumstances and the area were new

to us. Later on, we became familiar with landfalls and got more used to the fatigue.

There was no heating in the Catalina and we had to rely on thick clothing for warmth. The pilots and blister gunners wore sheepskin Irvin suits over several layers of woollens, as well as fur-lined flying boots and three pairs of gloves. Tim used to tell us that his recipe for warmth was to wear a pair of silk pyjamas underneath his woollens. I found the Irvin suit too bulky for continuous movement about the aircraft and wore instead a one-piece Sidcot suit over several layers of woollens. I also wore three pairs of gloves but I had to take off the two outer ones, leather and woollen, and rely on the silk ones when using instruments and plotting on the chart. I also found the leather helmet too tight for comfort and preferred to wear two woollen Balaclavas, while keeping the helmet handy for plugging into the intercom when necessary. Thus I had to endure the continuous roar of the engines, but the onset of headaches and air-sickness was reduced.

The solid mass of pack ice continued almost as far as Jan Mayen Island, which we first sighted at 08.50 hours. Mount Beerenberg towered above us, up to 8,000 feet. This was a stark and foreboding mass of rock, with its upper reaches shrouded in cloud, but it presented us with a most welcome sight after our long journey. The field of polar pack ice ceased suddenly close to the island, but the surface of the sea was littered with large clusters of broken floes, separated by dark patches of clear water. We had become so used to appraising different types of ice conditions that this was no longer fearsome. Instead, it seemed to us a scene of delightful serenity.

The pilots flew visually round the western side of the island and one could sense a general lifting of morale throughout the aircraft. It was not merely the impressive view. We had made another safe landfall after a long flight and were about to start on the last leg, to Iceland. The ice would soon be left behind and the temperature would improve. We had been in the air for 19 hours, but the next 300 miles should be easier flying. Ronnie Martin recollects his first sight of Jan Mayen Island.

It was quite an amazing sight as it stuck up out of field ice on the north side, with drift ice on the south side. This was the only time we saw it in clear visibility. On all the other occasions we passed

the island, it was covered in cloud almost down to sea level. The
Norwegians had set up a weather and radio station on the island,
and we were told that they had heard at least two German aircraft
crash on the peak in bad weather. They found only one of these,
for the other was too high up the peak. Their navigators could not
have been as good as our Scho, for we never had any problem.

The edge of the drift ice ran in a south-westerly direction from Jan
Mayen Island, and we followed this until it curved away to the west.
Our ice reconnaissance was then complete and we turned to port for
our destination.

Most of the fuel had been consumed and the aircraft was lighter.
The combination of a higher airspeed and a light following wind
brought our ground speed up to 114 knots, the highest throughout
the flight. We had had the misfortune of making a lefthand circuit
round an anti-cyclone, with head winds all the way. The last signal
we had received included 'AKUREYRI FIT', but it lay at the southern
end of Eyja fjord, about 40 miles from the open sea, with the
possibility of fog.

The sea was glassy calm and the wind negligible. There was little
for me to do and I switched places with Ronnie, sitting in the second
pilot's seat, chatting to Tim about our forthcoming reports and
adjusting the automatic pilot. Iceland was sighted at 12.10 hours
and we arrived gratifyingly close to our dead-reckoning position.
Ronnie returned to his seat and we were waterborne at 13.50 hours,
mooring up 20 minutes later.

We had been in the air for over 23 hours. The cessation of engine
noise brought a sudden transition to intense silence, broken only by
the lapping of wavelets against the hull. There was also the glow of
satisfaction of a job well done, for we felt we had achieved all that was
humanly possible in the weather conditions.

Our hosts were the Norwegians of 330 squadron, based at
Akureyri with their Northrop N-3PB floatplanes, also part of
Coastal Command. They were marvellously hospitable, recognised
that we needed food and sleep, and never once questioned us about
our unexpected arrival.

We made a preliminary report for Coastal Command and the
Admiralty. Sandy and Dan took all their equipment ashore, apart
from the dinghy, and departed in a jaunty mood to join Operation
Fritham. Before leaving, they both wrote letters to Group Captain

Dicken of the Special Operations Planning Section at Coastal Command Headquarters, complimenting our crew on the effectiveness of the flight.*

Akureyri is the second largest town in Iceland, and I was delighted to buy a teddy bear and a length of silk dress material for our baby daughter. She was only two months old and, needless to say, was the main topic in the letters exchanged between Hattie and myself. We left Iceland at 09.05 hours on 8 May and were moored up at Sullom Voe six hours later. Detailed reports were sent to Coastal Command Headquarters and the Admiralty the following day.

*See Appendix I

CHAPTER FOUR

On Our Own

The experience of our first ice reconnaissance had justified Tim's rejection of Catalina W8428, but we still needed a better aircraft to continue our Arctic flights. Another trip to the maintenance base at Gourock was arranged, but beforehand Tim had a long discussion with our squadron commander, Wing Commander Hutton. After this, a signal was sent to Coastal Command Headquarters notifying them that our crew was being flown to Gourock to inspect and report on the suitability of an aircraft for this task. When we arrived there, on 10 May 1942, the maintenance staff had obviously received instructions from a high level.

In the event, it was eleven days before we were able to return to Sullom Voe, for many other important visits took place in that period. Tim was instructed to report to Coastal Command Headquarters at Northwood for a personal briefing about the events that lay ahead, and to bring his navigator with him. Thus, I was soon to learn about the operation, but meanwhile Tim remained tight-lipped.

We travelled to London by train and spent an evening and a night in transit accommodation. During the evening, Tim and I were writing letters in an otherwise deserted room. Tim needed an envelope, but declined my offer of a white one. He said that it must be a blue one since, according to a simple code he had devised with his wife, a blue envelope meant that it did not contain any bad news. I was about to go upstairs to our room and he asked me to bring down a blue envelope from his briefcase. To my surprise, he handed me his keys, although it was not usually his custom to lock his briefcase. I wondered if it contained something confidential about the operations.

The envelopes were on the top of his papers and I picked up a blue one. Alongside them were two copies of the *Geographical Journal*, which was not the sort of periodical I would have expected Tim to read. Moreover, there were red crosses against two of the articles listed on the outer covers of these journals, which reminded me of our teacher's practice at school. I read the titles. In Volume LXII of 1923, there was 'The Magnetic Variation in the Neighbourhood of the North Pole, page 419', while in Volume XCI of 1938 there was 'Drift of the Soviet Polar Camp, page 156'.

It seemed obvious that Tim wanted me to see these articles and that this was his way of passing a message without breaching his orders to maintain strict secrecy. I picked up the two journals and thumbed through the articles, noting a chart on page 476 entitled 'Lines of Force and Curves of Equal Magnetic Variation in the neighbourhood of the North Pole'. The implications were shattering. The North Pole!

I replaced the journals, locked the case and returned downstairs, intending Tim to make the next move. He was stretched out in front of a large fireplace trying to get some warmth from a one-bar electric fire. He was looking at a picture, a well-known painting which depicted the gallant Captain Oates on Scott's last expedition to the South Pole. Staggering out of the tent, with his body bent against the force of the blizzard, he was accepting the inevitability of a frozen death in the hope that by sharing his rations the remainder of the group might survive to reach the next food depot. I handed the envelope to Tim and joined him in studying the painting.

At last, Tim broke the silence.

'If you were out there on the ice pack and a blizzard was blowing, and you wanted to go to the toilet, and there wasn't a toilet to go to, how would you avoid getting frostbite?'*

Tim was adept at making light-hearted comments about awkward situations, and I expected him to be laughing. It came as a shock to see that he was serious. He had meant it! The room began to feel colder.

He started talking again, choosing his words carefully.

'When they tell you what they have in mind, you'll think they've gone mad. I did at first. But after talking to Sandy, I'm hooked on the idea. You're more rational. You might want to have nothing to do with it. If you want to opt out, you don't have to say so. When they ask you whether it can be done, all you have to do is say "No". Then they'll drop the idea.'

'Why do they want me to tell them?' I asked. 'Don't they know?'

---

*Although, of course, discussions of so long ago cannot be quoted verbatim, the conversations in this book represent the events accurately as well as the spirit with which they took place.

'No, they don't,' laughed Tim. 'It's never been done before by the RAF. They want to know whether we can do it, and you seem to be the only one who can tell them.'

'You must have talked to Wing Commander Hutton about it. What happened then?' I asked.

'I said that if any navigator in the squadron could do it, you could,' replied Tim, with a broad smile.

'Thanks a lot,' I said, but did not return his smile. I did not like all this banter about what was clearly a most difficult project. It seemed to me time to do some straight talking.

'Am I to understand that they want to know whether we can take our Catalina right over the Knob?'*

But Tim was not to be drawn. 'I can't tell you about the operation. But let me put it this way. We both know that the first duty of a reconnaissance crew is to return to base. Without asking where that base will be, just suppose that we were to find ourselves over the Pole. If that happened to us, would we be able to bring our Catalina back to base? If you can answer that question, you'll tell them what they want to know. It's a tricky one, and a bit too complex for me, but it's right up your street. I thought that you ought to have some time to think about it before talking to them tomorrow. We're not only going to be briefed. They want to know whether it can be done.'

Tim was now his cheerful self again, as though a load had been lifted from his mind. He picked up his letter and turned towards the door.

'I'm going to bed,' he said. 'We shall have to be on the ball tomorrow, so don't stay up too late.'

'If you want to scribble down a few notes, these might help,' was his parting comment. He gave me a few sheets of his blue notepaper. I didn't miss the point. It was so typical of Tim. Nor was I fooled about 'just happening' to find ourselves over the Pole. Ice reconnaissances, Dan and Sandy, Spitsbergen, and the need for a reliable aircraft - they all pointed in one direction. I had to think about how to get there as well as how to get back.

It did not take long to list the problems that would have to be solved. Indeed, all our experienced squadron navigators could have pin-pointed them. All I had to do was to envisage being in an aircraft over the Pole, as Tim had suggested, and to consider what the next action would be under normal aircraft procedures.

*'The Knob' was RAF slang for the North Pole.

Most schoolboys know that if you keep on flying northwards you will eventually reach the North Pole. But when you turn round to fly home, it is no use saying 'fly due south', because *all* directions from the North Pole lead southwards. It seemed to me that a different method of describing direction would be needed.

An obvious solution was to describe the direction of Greenwich from the Pole as zero and all other directions in a 360 degree circle from that. Such a technique was already in use for astro-navigation in the concept of 'Greenwich Hour Angle' (GHA), the celestial equivalent of the angular difference between the Greenwich meridian and that of a heavenly body, measured in a clockwise direction around the Pole. To avoid confusion with GHA, perhaps the terrestial direction could be referred to as degrees Greenwich or some similar term. This would cover the whole of the polar region, not just at the Pole itself.

Having selected a method of describing direction and explained it to the pilots, what instruments could they use to ensure that the aircraft was on the correct course? Would a magnetic compass be effective so close to the North Magnetic Pole* and, if so, what sort? The magnetic compasses in regular use in the RAF were designed for lower latitudes, where the horizontal strength of the earth's magnetic field was far greater. Was any information available about the relative strengths of the horizontal and vertical components of the earth's magnetic field in polar regions?

Perhaps the distant-reading gyro-magnetic compass would be effective in the far north. But even if suitable magnetic compasses could be made available, what adjustments would have to be made to convert their magnetic directions to true directions? The chart on page 476 of the *Geographical Journal* for 1923, giving magnetic variation, would have to be studied more carefully.

Assuming that magnetic compasses were used for only the more southerly part of the journey, could astro compasses be used to guide the aircraft to and from the Pole? These depended on astronomical observations and not on the earth's magnetic field. If so, how many compasses would be needed and where could they be fitted? There was no astrodome in the Catalina, nor any position from which the sun could be seen continuously in all directions. Astro compasses could be fitted by the windows on either side of the pilots' cockpit,

---

*The North Magnetic Pole was then believed to be in the region of the Boothia Peninsula in Northern Canada.

but these were sometimes in the shade cast by the high wing. Could additional astro compasses be fitted in the blisters and, if so, could the pilots steer by their gyroscopes with periodic guidance from an observer in the blister compartment? We often used the astro compass to check the accuracy of a heading shown by a magnetic compass. To do this, settings had to be made on the instrument, for the latitude of the aircraft and the 'declination' and 'hour angle' of the sun.* The result of these settings was that the sun's rays caused a marker bar on the compass to cast a shadow against guide lines on the opposite side of the instrument, so that the true course of the aircraft could be read against a lubber line. However, the sun moves by one degree of hour angle every four minutes, so that remote control from the blister compartment would have to be continuous and would require much planning and preparatory training. Also, quite obviously, the method could not be used at all unless the sun remained visible during this part of the flight.

Once direction measurement and course steering had been settled, what sort of chart would be needed for plotting the aircraft's position? We were accustomed to using Mercator charts, on which lines of latitude and longitude were represented as straight and parallel lines at right angles to each other. Obviously, such a chart could not be used to depict the North Pole, where all lines of longitude had to meet. Some of the land masses in the Arctic region were about 600 miles from the Pole. It seemed desirable to construct a chart of the polar region on a blank sheet of paper, with a dot in the centre representing the Pole and the 80th parallel touching the outer edges, together with a few coastlines suitably marked. Then meridians of longitude would radiate outwards from the Pole, like the spokes of a wheel, while parallels of latitude would be represented by concentric circles. Several types of map projection of this type could be devised, each having different charactersics for dead-reckoning navigation, as modified for polar flying.

One problem would be to determine how far apart the concentric circles of latitude should be. There were changes of scale on the normal Mercator chart, but these could be far more complex on a polar projection. On a 'polar gnomonic' projection, scale varied

---

*Declination is the latitude of a sub-stellar point, measured from the centre of the earth to the heavenly body. Hour angle is the longitude of the heavenly body, measured westwards from a datum point through 360 degrees.

along the meridians, but how accurately could distances be measured along routes which crossed several meridians? It might be desirable to avoid crossing meridians and to fly only in north-south directions. This would have to be related to the purpose of the reconnaissance, but this had not been explained to me.

It was getting late, and my mind was probably seeking relief from these complexities. I reminded myself that our two passengers were holders of the Polar Medal. Explorers were said to seek their objectives simply because 'they were there'. I wondered if some senior officers in the RAF were motivated by similar ideas. Did someone want to score a notable first - in the middle of a war?

It became clear to me that, at some stage in a flight to the Pole, we would have to change from one technique to another. The Admiralty chart of the Greenland and Barents Seas, based on the normal Mercator projection, extended as far as the latitude of 82 degrees North. The northernmost land masses of Peary Land, Greenland, Spitsbergen and Franz Josef Land had coastlines between 80 and 83 degrees North. We should be able to use normal methods of navigation to such departure points, and change to polar navigation techniques from there northwards.

Weather conditions would have special significance for a polar flight. Our first ice reconnaissance had demonstrated the need to avoid patches of moist air to minimise the danger of aircraft icing. The absence of meteorological stations in the polar region would diminish the reliability of any forecasts. Would we have to rely on our own observations, such as noting cloud formations, wind changes, pressure readings and changes of visibility? We could not safely set course from a departure point without the certainty of good weather ahead of us in the polar basin. To permit the measurement of wind velocity by taking drifts, we would have to see the surface of the ice below the aircraft. To make use of astro compasses and obtain position lines from observation of the sun, clear skies would be needed above the aircraft. We would have to turn back at the first sign of heavy cloud or fog.

This line of reasoning brought to attention the most desirable timing for a polar flight. Measurement of the altitude of the sun, by a marine or RAF bubble sextant, provided the navigator with a position line at right angles to the direction of the sun. It would take the Catalina about six hours to fly from 80 degrees North to the North Pole, and another six hours to come back. If we set course from somewhere near the 80th parallel when the sun was above the eastern horizon, the position line would confirm the longitude of our departure point. When we neared the Pole, the position line would be athwart our track and thus indicate whether we had reached our objective. On the return journey, the position line would indicate whether we were close to the required longitude, particularly as we neared the 80th parallel.

I wondered whether there was any indication about how others had navigated over the polar ice. Would any precautions have to be taken against snow and ice blindness? If we were compelled to make a forced landing, was any information available about safety and rescue? Why did they want us to do it anyway? There were many questions to be asked, but it was time to go to bed, although there was not much of the night left for sleep. I gathered up my notes and sketches, took one last look at Captain Oates, and went upstairs.

We arrived at Coastal Command Headquarters with time to spare on the following morning. A senior officer popped his head around the door of the room while we were waiting.

'Are you the captain and navigator of the Catalina? What a marvellous adventure! How I wish I were thirty years younger! Lucky devils! Good luck!'

His head disappeared without further explanation. Another officer appeared at the door. He was also enthusiastic, but his comments included 'twenty years younger'. Then a junior officer passed through the room. Tim's chiding reference to 'five years younger' received a brusque response.

'Wouldn't touch it with a barge pole. Some people don't seem to realise there's supposed to be a war on.' We gained the impression that he was much too busy to devote time to us.

Tim just sat there with a benign look on his face, confident that he could cope with anything that might arise. Then Group Captain C.W. Dicken came in. He explained that he was in charge of the Special Operations Section at Headquarters. I was under the impression that our captain had never met him before, but he treated Tim as an old friend. In no time at all, out came the direct question:

'Can you do it?'

Tim was in a happy, teasing mood. 'Scho knows nothing about Operation Fritham and I know very little. With respect, sir, don't you think it would be a good idea to tell us what this is all about, before asking whether we can do it?'

We all laughed, and the Group Captain congratulated Tim on

security. We then retired to the more confidential surroundings of his room, where he explained the background to Operation Fritham. When he got round to the subject of the flight to the North Pole, I learned that this would take place from an advanced base in Spitsbergen. To achieve this, 6,000 gallons of petrol, 250 gallons of oil and the necessary maintenance equipment were to be taken to Spitsbergen as soon as the expedition had established a firm foothold.

He mentioned that the experts hoped to derive enough information from all the ice reconnaissances to forecast the movements of ice through the three outflow channels. We were also told that Air Chief Marshal Sir Philip Joubert and Air Vice-Marshal Baker gave the plan whole-hearted support. I still did not understand why a flight to the Pole was required to help forecast the movements of the ice pack 1,000 miles away. However, I was not knowledgeable in such matters, and if the Commander-in-Chief and the Admiralty thought that the flight was necessary, who was I to question it? Everyone else seemed to think it was a good idea. I could feel my own enthusiasm rising to meet the challenge. Tim had been right!

Dicken acknowledged that flights beyond the 80th parallel would be very hazardous. He emphasised that there could be no air-sea rescue service. He also stressed that Headquarters did not intend to *order* a polar flight to be carried out. The captain of the Catalina would be given unfettered authority, as well as the sole command over the remainder of the aircrew. Tim would be junior in rank to other leaders of the expedition but not subordinate to them. He alone would decide what the RAF contribution should be, in respect to all flights he carried out for Operation Fritham. He would hold his authority direct from the Commander-in-Chief. If he had to make use of that authority in order to preserve secrecy or to achieve results, he should handle any senior officers as tactfully as possible. But, if necessary, any outraged officers could be referred to Headquarters. Then the Group Captain came back to his first question:

'Can you do it?'

Tim was happy to leave this part of the talking to me. I brought out all the questions that had occurred to me during the previous evening. It soon became clear that the Special Operations Section had already given some thought to the subject, for most of the unresolved questions seemed to tally. Dicken admitted that he could not answer many of the questions, but said that he hoped to arrange introductions to various experts outside the RAF who might help. We were again reminded that we were to say nothing about Operation Fritham, nothing about the advanced base in Spitsbergen, and nothing about the ice-cap. He did not know how we could ask questions about polar navigation without talking about flying to the North Pole, but Tim assured him that this would present no problem.

Group Captain Dicken was able to allocate to us the whole of the remainder of the morning, as we continued our discussion. He then told us that there were six days available to search for answers elsewhere. Afterwards, our Catalina had to be picked up from the Clyde. After that, he said, everything could be summarised in one sentence:

'You'll be on your own!'

Our allocation of time ran out shortly before lunchtime. There remained only one further item at Headquarters, a discussion with Air Vice Marshal G.B.A. Baker. He was brief and to the point. Once again, security was stressed and Tim was told that he was in sole command. The Air Vice Marshal was enthusiastic, confident and full of assurance, but also cautious.

'Remember that there's no rescue service up there, so turn back before it's too late. We shan't complain. Whatever decisions you take will receive one hundred per cent support from this Headquarters.'

His parting message was:

'You'll be on your own. Good luck!'

It seemed that they really meant it.

The first call arranged by Group Captain Dicken was at the Hydrography Department of the Admiralty, in search of polar charts. We had decided that the 'hour angle' method of describing direction, clockwise round the Pole, was the best method for our purposes. Dicken had drawn our attention to a treatise written by Squadron Leader K.C. Maclure of the RCAF, in which he shortened degrees 'Greenwich' to degrees 'G' and recommended its use over the whole of the polar basin. We had agreed to adopt this. Directions in degrees 'G' could be reconciled with degrees 'T' (True) and degrees 'M' (Magnetic) by the use of a simple conversion formula.* But Dicken had not been able to find any polar charts in RAF archives, for apparently the need for them had not arisen previously.

We were escorted through a maze of corridors in the Admiralty to

*See Appendix III

the correct department. I cannot remember the rank of the officer we saluted, but he had many rings on his sleeve and remained seated. I had the impression he was an admiral. He evidently disapproved of me at first, since I was wearing a forage cap instead of a peaked cap.

Tim began by name-dropping and buttering-up. We had come from Coastal Command Headquarters where the Air Chief Marshal was seeking ways to improve the assistance we could give to vessels on the Russian convoy route. We were planning some long-range reconnaissance work along the southern edge of the polar ice field and might be compelled to fly beyond the Mercator charts currently provided by the RAF. Did the Royal Navy have in its archives any maps of the polar region which we could use?

'I presume that you mean charts,' was the rather frosty response.

They did not have much use for maps at the Admiralty, since these mainly represented the topography of land masses and were of little use when navigating over the sea. Tim had made a gaffe and duly put in his place, but it took more than that to dismay him.

The high-ranking naval officer was also adept at dropping names. Apparently our C-in-C had already had a word with him, and some charts had been selected. He asked his 'number one' to bring them in. So far, I had kept in the background, but I found it difficult to curb my enthusiasm when 'number one' came back into the room. He was holding one of the charts by the corners and it was so stiff that it stuck out horizontally in front of him. We did not have paper of that quality in the RAF.

The charts were spread out on a table, and Tim seemed at a loss for words. It was obviously time for me to take part, for surely not even an admiral could object to a navigator taking a look. One of them was Admiralty chart 260. This was a 'Zenithal Equidistant' projection, with the North Pole at the centre and extending as far south as the 50th degree of latitude at its outer edges. It gave a good representation of the area we would be covering from Britain northwards and would be useful for planning routes, but the scale was far too small for air navigation.

The stiff chart was far more interesting. This was Admiralty chart 5030, entitled 'Polar Regions'. This was a 'gnomonic' projection, about three feet by two feet six inches, with the Pole offset to about six inches from one edge. Lines of latitude were at two degree intervals, with lines of longitude at every five degrees as far as 85 degrees North and then at wider intervals nearer the Pole. It was otherwise blank, with no land masses at all, so that it could be used in either the Arctic or the Antarctic.

We looked at the charts in silence, broken only by the terse comment that Admiralty charts were printed on only one side, when I lifted a corner to take a quick peek underneath. I explained that we already used normal Admiralty charts, on a Mercator projection, as far as 80 degrees North, but that the blank chart 5030 could be of great use beyond that. Then I asked if it would be possible for this chart to be marked with any land masses that crossed the 80th parallel.

Tim told me afterwards that he didn't know if there were any land masses that crossed the 80th parallel, and so kept quiet. The thought occurred to me at the time that perhaps the naval officers didn't know either. The silence was broken when 'number one' asked permission to find out how busy his hydrographers were.

'Yes, it can be done,' he said, on returning. 'Which coastlines do you require?'

Perhaps he was trying to turn the tables on me. Tim looked relieved when I replied, 'Peary Land, Greenland, Spitsbergen and Franz Josef Land.'

We took the other charts with us. The redrawn chart would be sent to our C-in-C, three days later. As soon as we had been escorted out of the august premises, Tim stopped being serious.

'The next time we go to the Admiralty, you'd better not wear a forage cap!'

'The next time we go to the Admiralty, you'd better not ask for a map!' I countered.

'Next time, you shouldn't look at the wrong side of a chart!'

'Oh yes, I shall. Didn't you notice the quality of the paper? We can draw an equidistant projection on the back, and if the 80th parallel has the same radius as on their gnomonic chart, we can copy the coastlines from their chart to ours.'

'Cheeky devil!' said Tim, but there was a note of approval in his voice.

The next visit on that day was to a gyro manufacturer in the London area. We had already discussed compasses and gyros with Group Captain Dicken. There were three compasses in the Catalina. Two of these were the standard magnetic compasses, the P4 fitted on the floor below the captain, and the smaller P9 which was usually fitted above the pilots' heads and viewed through a mirror. High-latitude versions of these two compasses had been arranged for us and were due for delivery at Northwood before the end of the week. The third compass was the distant-reading gyro-magnetic, which was considered to be the most effective although it sometimes suffered from electrical faults which caused the repeater dials to move out of synchronisation with the master unit in the tail. The Royal Aircraft Establishment had given the opinion that the DR compass might be effective as far as 85 degrees North, but the experts were not absolutely certain about this since there would be increased friction at the double pivot as the horizontal strength of the earth's magnetic field diminished. We also wanted to find out if the standard gyro in the pilots' instrument panel could be improved upon; perhaps a manufacturer could produce an instrument of exceptionally good quality.

As we expected, the gyro manufacturer confirmed that a perfect gyro could not be produced, but some were better than others. He offered us two which had performed well on the test bed. But directional gyros fitted to aircraft wandered and precessed, and the manufacturer warned us that the rate was unpredictable. While we were there, Tim was induced to give a 'pep talk' to some of the staff in the canteen, where we were given a meal. They enjoyed it, and so did he.

There was just enough time left in the day to visit an Army unit specialising in alpine and Arctic warfare. We had already discussed how we might try to cope on the ice if we were stranded. The two ice observers were to fly with us on all the forthcoming reconnaissances, but we were not very confident about our ability to live off the land without their guidance. We should have to use a sporting rifle and fishing lines, and had been told to supplement our normal emergency rations with a good supply of pemmican, margarine and vitamin C tablets. In addition, although our flying boots were warm they were not suitable for walking across ice. We hoped that the Army unit might be able to supply us with such items as boots, sleeping bags and sun glasses.

The Army men proved very keen to help, and they politely refrained from asking which glacier or mountain we intended to climb. They offered us several pairs of boots of assorted sizes, all large so that we could wear several pairs of socks. They also gave us a dozen sleeping bags and three dozen pairs of goggles with different types of tinted glass. They suggested that we experiment with the latter to find out if some were not successful. We thanked them, and promised to let them know the result.

Early the next morning, we set off to find the wartime abode of the Astronomer Royal, Harold Spencer Jones. The headquarters of the

Royal Greenwich Observatory had moved to Abinger Hammer in Surrey. It was believed that here we would find the leading authority on the state of the earth's magnetic field in the Arctic. Enquiries were also being made at this establishment about the provision of chronometer watches specially designed for use at low temperatures.

Our driver was a young WAAF who had recently passed her driving test. She successfully crossed the Thames Valley but became lost in the Surrey hills where, of course, all the signposts had been removed. The woodlands around Abinger Hammer were being used as bomb storage depots, and Tim commented on the peculiarity of the British in removing the Astronomer Royal from the danger of air raids and surrounding him with bombs. Eventually, the young lady turned round in despair and enquired:

'Can either of you two gentlemen map-read?'

Tim exercised his considerable charm and obliged.

Unfortunately Mr Jones was not at home, but his assistant had been well briefed. A long discussion resulted in the conclusion that there was no better information than the article we had already seen in the *Geographical Journal*. These estimates of magnetic variation were not quite as reliable as those on the charts further south, but were likely to be accurate enough for our purposes. It was reassuring to talk to an expert, and we enjoyed the outing.

On returning to London, there was time for a short visit to the Headquarters of the Royal Norwegian forces, to collect some maps of Spitsbergen that they had prepared for us. As we went in, a large man was leaving, carrying a huge rucksack on his back and skis over his shoulder. This was a somewhat unusual sight in wartime London. We gathered from a casual comment that he would be traversing a glacier in the far north of Norway on the following day. Evidently someone else was 'on his own'.

The final suggestion made by Group Captain Dicken had not occurred to me, but it proved to be the most productive of the week. This was a two-day visit to Cambridge, to browse through the archives of the Scott Polar Research Institute. Tim had been given a letter of introduction to the master of St John's College, J.M. Wordie, who was also in charge of the Institute. I was happy to explain that I had been a scholar at this college six years previously and that I knew Mr Wordie well, having enjoyed some boat club breakfasts with him. A further appointment had been made with Professor Debenham at the Faculty of Geography.

Mr Wordie and his assistants seemed to know what was needed without having to ask any probing questions. Nevertheless, there was a remarkable shortage of information about how others had navigated by air over the polar ice. We were told how to build an igloo, the advantages of the Nansen-type sledge, and relevant matters concerning survival. It was all very interesting.

On the following day we visited the Faculty of Geography, and spent some long and rewarding sessions with its head, Professor Frank Debenham, who was also a founder member of the Scott Polar Institute. Dr Debenham must have been well briefed by Group Captain Dicken. Although neither Tim nor I mentioned the purpose of our mission, a discussion in the privacy of the professor's home concentrated precisely on the problems which were exercising our minds.

The professor recommended strongly that we should use a 'polar equidistant' projection. After enquiring about the size of the navigation table, he decided that the scale of the chart should be 30 nautical miles to the inch, so that the lines of latitude would be two inches apart. He arranged for three of his research assistants, all charming young ladies, to draw up a chart for us on this basis.

He had also prepared some typed notes under the heading of 'Position Line Navigation Near To The Pole', and went through these step by step. Each line of reasoning started from a basic principle of astro-navigation but was then related to practical application. He showed us the advantages to be gained from sun sights, both on the approach to the Pole and for determining position when precisely at the Pole.* We benefited enormously from the tutorial experience of a man whose academic researches were continued into such practical application.

Tim and I returned to London with much to think about but no conclusions to report to Group Captain Dicken. We collected all our instruments, charts, papers, and our kit, and then caught a crowded train to Glasgow. The compartment was locked, much to the indignation of those standing in the corridor, but we were too concerned about the security of our belongings to give way to their scowls.

Ronnie and the other members of the crew were delighted to see us. Our new Catalina, serial VA 729, letter 'P for Peter', looked so beautiful that no one wanted to miss the opportunity of flying away in it. We returned to Sullom Voe on 21 May.

*See Appendix III

CHAPTER FIVE

Operation Fritham

While Tim and I had been enjoying a week of enlightenment and relaxation in the south of England, Operation Fritham had been getting under way further north. The Norwegian Navy had made available the icebreaker *Isbjørn* of 437 tons and the sealer *Selis* of 166 tons.

The two vessels sailed from Greenock in the Clyde on 30 April 1942, under the command of Lieutenant Øi of the Royal Norwegian Navy. They carried a landing party of about 60 Norwegians, mostly ex-miners who had been evacuated from Spitsbergen in the autumn of 1941 and whose military training had been minimal. These were commanded by Lieutenant-Colonel Einar Sverdrup, the director of Store Norske Spitsbergen Kulkompani Aktieselskap, the Norwegian coal-mining company at Longyearbyen; he had been brought away from Spitsbergen against his wishes. The total force, including the crews of the two ships, amounted to about 85 men. All were eager to return home, were willing to endure their cramped quarters, and were glad to be active again after a period of enforced idleness. In conventional military terms, they could not be considered a trained assault force, but events were to prove that they possessed qualities which seasoned troops might envy.

The regular monitoring of German wireless messages and their decrypting at Bletchley Park had revealed that weather reconnaissance aircraft had made flights over Spitsbergen on 26 and 27 April. It was this information which caused the last-minute amendment to our flight of 3 May, to include a reconnaissance of Icefjord and an attempt to put Glen and Godfrey ashore at Cape Linné. The information that an enemy unit was in Spitsbergen, probably at Quade Hock in Kings Bay, was passed to Sverdrup on the day before the vessels sailed. Since Kings Bay had been one of the possible landing places for the expedition, it was decided to make for Icefjord. Here it might be possible to land at Green Harbour, even if the eastern part of the fjord was still icebound.

The two ships were of sound construction, although old and slow. However, there were two serious deficiencies for an expedition of this nature. One was that, although each ship was fitted with an Oerlikon gun, there were no trained gun crews. The other was that the wireless equipment was in a poor state of repair and inadequate for long-range communication. Major A.B. Whatman of the Royal Corps of Signals was one of the three British liaison officers who sailed with the expedition. When he went aboard on 28 April, he was dismayed to find the wireless unserviceable and without regular operators. He repaired the set himself and was forced to act as operator for some of the time. Even so, there was little likelihood that it could transmit or receive messages from the UK once the ships had passed beyond Jan Mayen Island. In fact the equipment was fully serviceable only for the first part of their journey, to Akureyri on the north coast of Iceland.

At Akureyri the other two liaison officers, Glen and Godfrey, boarded the vessels; we had landed them there on 4 May. They picked up further supplies and set sail on 8 May. Glen took with him a copy of the ice report which he and Tim had prepared three days earlier. This demonstrated that the route had to be further east than intended, but the vessels sailed as far to the north as the ice permitted. We know now that the German reconnaissance flights were usually east-west, between North Cape of Norway and Jan Mayen Island, with an occasional diversion from Jan Mayen to South Cape of Spitsbergen. There was thus little risk of the expedition being spotted, after it had passed to the north-east of Jan Mayen.

While the Norwegians in London were planning to return to their Spitsbergen homeland, four German meteorologists at Bansö were also preparing to make a move, but for different reasons. They were all anxious to end their long winter isolation, and in fact one of them was showing signs of polar psychosis. While the spring thaw improved the chances of a successful landing by the Norwegians, it would give the Germans an opportunity to depart. Transport facilities for both parties improved as the sun rose higher in the sky each day.

Those German meteorologists who had been taken to Spitsbergen by the trawlers, sealers and U-boats, expected to be taken out by the same method.* However, the Bansö station had been set up by the

*In fact, the members of the 'Knospe' station at Lilliehöökfjord were hastily evacuated by *U-435* in August 1942, after being attacked by a small party of Norwegians.

Luftwaffe, and their relief also had to be by air. The evacuation of personnel and their replacement by automatic equipment was entirely in the hands of the weather reconnaissance airmen flying from Vaernes and Banak in Norway.

The evacuation by air posed problems which were rather different from those which the German pilots faced when the station was set up the previous autumn. Then, there had been frequent flights by He111s, Ju88s and Ju52s, and the pilots became aware of the problems presented by soft ground, ruts and boulders. It was even more difficult to cope with these hazards when they were hidden by soft snow. Moreover, although frozen ground and bay ice could provide an airstrip as hard as a concrete runway, the snow on top of it created a major problem. Deep snow could bring a sudden halt to the forward movement of an aircraft, tipping its nose forward or slewing the aircraft around. It could also prevent the aircraft gaining enough momentum to reach a safe take-off speed. When using the ice as a runway, weaknesses such as those caused by a thin layer over a seal hole might not be seen. The results could be damage to undercarriages and propellers.

The German ground parties usually reported when conditions seemed favourable for a landing, but it was the pilot who had to make the final decision. This called for a careful inspection of the airstrip at low level, before making an approach at as slow a speed as possible. The method was not dissimilar to that of flying boats, when pilots made a close inspection before landing on the open sea.

On 2 May, wireless and meteorological equipment had arrived at Banak for the installation of an automatic weather station at Bansö, under the supervision of Dr Fritz Woelfle. The equipment was contained in a metal box, which the airmen called a 'Kröte' (Toad) after their squadron motif. The early models consisted essentially of a thermometer, a barometer, a wireless transmitter, and batteries capable of providing sufficient power for several months of operation. The later models included more sophisticated equipment. But this 'Kröte' was intended for delivery to Spitsbergen as soon as weather conditions proved favourable. After it began to work satisfactorily, the ground party would be evacuated.

The Luftwaffe had to wait for ten days before Bansö reported that conditions had improved sufficiently for a landing to be attempted. Then two aircraft set off from Banak, an He111 flown by Leutnant Rudolf Schütze and a Ju88 with Leutnant Heinz Wagner at the controls. They were carrying heavy loads of supplies, together with

A Ju88A of 'Wettererkundungsstaffel 5' taking off from Banak in northern Norway. This was photographed in 1943.

An He111 of 'Wettererkundungsstaffel 5' on the ice near Longyearbyen during Operation 'Bansö' in May 1942.

(*Left*) '*Kröte*' automatic weather station. This is being set up on Edge Island in Spitsbergen by the Germans in 1943.

(*Below*) '*Kröte*' automatic weather station being set up on Bear Island by the Germans in October 1942.

meteorologists and technicians to install and test the new equipment. Included in the party were Dr Etienne and Dr Woelfle.

When the aircraft arrived over Bansö, at 05.45 hours on 13 May, Wagner circled while Schütze attempted a landing. Schütze made a preliminary series of sweeps at low level over the landing strip, to inspect the surface. All seemed well. He brought his Heinkel gradually lower until the wheels brushed grooves in the snow without making contact with the ground beneath. Again, all seemed well. On the next approach, he used a 'fly on' technique, keeping the tailwheel off the snow and landing gently on the strip.

At first, the landing seemed to be successful, but the snow that built up in front of the wheels produced a violent braking effect. To the alarm of all on board, the nose dipped down and the tail flipped up. But Schütze managed to keep control and the Heinkel slewed round to a halt.

The crew were relieved to find that their aircraft was undamaged, but a difficult problem remained. Against such accumulations of snow, would Schütze be able to achieve the required speed for take-off?

There was a general atmosphere of jubilation as the ground party came forward to greet the ten men who jumped down from the Heinkel, the first visitors for six months. Schütze's first action was to fire Very Light signals to Wagner, warning him not to attempt a landing but to return to Banak. Leutnant Wagner had seen everything as he circled, and he had no hesitation in complying. After assuring himself that all were safe on the ground below, he turned and headed back over the mountains on the direct route to Banak. No sooner had Wagner's Ju88 disappeared over the southern horizon than the men on the ground heard the drone of another aircraft approaching from the north. It was an RAF Catalina, however, flying from the direction of Icefjord.

Since Sverdrup and Glen had not been able to report any sign of enemy activity after their flight over Spitsbergen at the beginning of April, the planners of Operation Fritham had possibly felt that the project was unlikely to be subjected to enemy interference. However, it was obviously desirable that another reconnaissance should be carried out before the expedition arrived, especially since thick fog had prevented us from landing Glen and Godfrey at Cape Linné on 4 May. Moreover, the Admiralty needed up-to-date information about the position of the southern edge of the Arctic icepack, in order to plan the next convoy to Russia. On 10 May it was decided to make a further reconnaissance of Icefjord, Cape Linné and Advent Bay, as well as a review of the sea ice between Bear Island and Spitsbergen, and from there towards Jan Mayen Island, with particular reference to the area west of Bear Island in the region of latitude 74 degrees North.

Our squadron was instructed to carry out this flight not later than 12 May. Since our aircraft was not yet ready and Tim and I were on our 'grand tour' in search of polar expertise, the reconnaissance was carried out by Flight Lieutenant G.G. Potier, with Pilot Officer R.J. Fairley as navigator. While they were airborne on 12 May, a wireless message from a German weather aircraft over Spitsbergen was intercepted; this must have come from either Schütze or Wagner, confirming their arrival in the area.

Potier's flight was carried out in a clockwise direction, from Muckle Flugga to Jan Mayen Island, to establish the position of the ice edge in the Greenland Sea, before completing the reconnaissance of Icefjord.* The crew first sighted Spitsbergen at a range of 38 miles. They then made a landfall at Bell Sound at 05.40 hours, five minutes before Rudolf Schütze arrived over Bansö. During the next 80 minutes, Dick Fairley was able to make only one entry in his navigator's log; during that time, he must have been in the blister compartment, taking photographs and recording the results of their reconnaissance. The report that the crew made on their return to Sullom Voe was a further example of meticulous workmanship.

The crew saw a pall of smoke over Barentsberg, but the hillside was in shadow and it was difficult to see the origin of the smoke. Their photographs of the buildings, mine workings and pylons confirmed their report that there were no tracks in the snow and no sign of any occupation. They saw pylons lying on their sides at Longyearbyen in Advent Bay, but no signs of human activity. However, towards the edge of the town they spotted two radio masts with tracks in the snow around some neighbouring buildings.

Ski tracks led the Catalina along the valley to a wide stretch of ground covered with snow. Here they saw an He111 with some men moving around it. The Catalina circled overhead, firing 1,500 rounds from the bow and blister machine guns. The gunners were sure that they had put the machine out of action and wounded or

* See Appendix II

Longyearbyen in Advent Bay, photographed from a Catalina of 210 Squadron captained by Flight Lieutenant G.G. Potier on 12 May 1942.

Green Harbour fjord photographed as Flight Lieutenant Potier flew eastwards along Icefjord on 12 May 1942. The bay ice extended round Cape Heer into Icefjord. Smoke was rising from Barentsberg, hidden in the shadow from the cliff behind the town.

ICEFJORD IN SPITSBERGEN

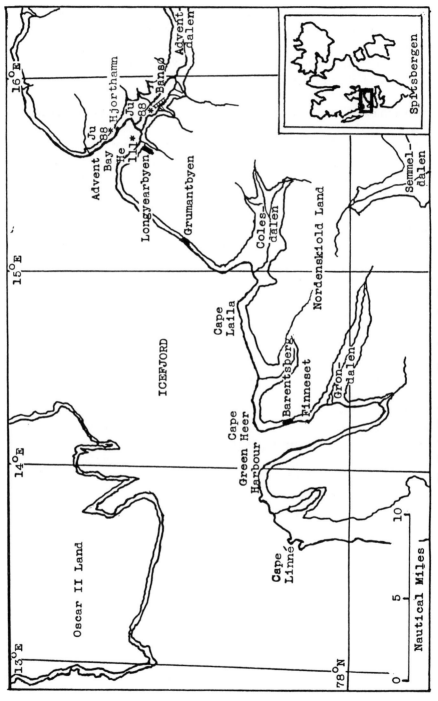

The line inside the coastline shows the 50 metre contour.

killed some of the Germans. Further photographs were taken of the site and the hut to which some of the men had run when the attack began.

The aircraft had been using richer mixture during the reconnaissance of Spitsbergen. Potier had been warned before take-off that they might be diverted to Invergordon or even Oban on return to base. Fuel supply was of special importance. As soon as he was satisfied that the Heinkel could not take off and give chase, Potier broke off the engagement and headed for Icefjord to begin the homeward journey. The reconnaissance around Bear Island had to be deleted from the itinerary. Instead, the Catalina headed straight for the Shetlands, and the crew eventually sighted North Unst at 16.00 hours. They landed at Sullom Voe and their report was made by phone to Coastal Command Headquarters, who immediately passed the information to the Admiralty. In turn, the Admiralty sent an urgent wireless signal to the *Isbjørn*, to warn the expedition of the enemy presence on Spitsbergen and alert Sverdrup to the danger from enemy aircraft.

After the Catalina had departed, Schütze was delighted to learn that none of the Germans had been hit. As the Norwegians were to learn two days later, it was surprising how little damage was inflicted on running men from gunfire sprayed sideways from a moving aircraft. The fourteen men were quite unharmed. On the other hand, the Heinkel had been pierced by about 30 bullets. There were holes in the pilot's windscreen, the fuselage, undercarriage, tail wheel, through a propeller blade and even in a fuel tank. No fuel had leaked out of the self-sealing tank and there had been no fire. A quick check revealed that both engines and all controls seemed to be in working order. Technically, the machine seemed still capable of flight. But there was still the problem of coping with the snow on take-off.

The unexpected attack by the Catalina and the possibility of a return visit spurred the men into rapid action. The precious cargo was off-loaded, none of it seriously damaged. Eight men stayed behind so that Schütze, in a lightened aircraft and accompanied only by a radio operator, could attempt the dangerous task of taking off.

It was necessary to convert the airstrip into a runway on which he could attain sufficient speed for take-off. Schütze taxied up and down the airstrip, keeping the wheels as close as he could to the same track but without making any deep ruts. The surface layer of the recently-fallen snow was whipped up into a cloud of fine particles by the exhausts, but the lower layers were gradually compacted into a hard surface. At first, it required maximum power just to move, but with each run the wheels turned more freely. After six runs, he was ready for the crucial test.

When the site had first been examined by Dr Etienne, the dip of the river terrace at the end of the runway had been regarded as a disadvantage. On this occasion, however, it gave the Heinkel just sufficient impetus to become airborne. Schütze climbed to operational height and headed southwards. His problems were not over, however. There was a cold draught from the holes in the windscreen, the starboard engine began to lose oil, and the radio equipment proved to be unserviceable. Nevertheless, he nursed the aircraft back to Banak, where it was found that the damage to the undercarriage and the tail unit was more serious than he had thought. But, even before Potier's report was studied at Coastal Command Headquarters, the machine he had attacked was undergoing repairs to bring it back into service.

Meanwhile, the *Isbjørn* and the *Selis* were approaching Spitsbergen. Early on the morning of 13 May, a look-out on the *Selis* thought he saw an aircraft low on the southern horizon. No sighting of the vessels can be traced in the records of the RAF or the Luftwaffe. It might have been Potier's Catalina, for the ships would have been difficult to spot in the low mist and the glow from the ice edge to the north of the aircraft.

The two ships arrived at the entrance to Icefjord at 20.00 hours on 13 May, without any knowledge of impending danger. The radio message from the Admiralty, warning them of the enemy presence should have reached them just in time. But we do not know exactly what happened. Perhaps the defective equipment was not manned at the time. The only comment that can be made is that the expedition could have been better equipped. One can only guess what action Sverdrup would have taken if the message had been picked up. Perhaps he would have headed northwards towards Magdalena Bay. Instead, attention was focussed on Cape Linné. A landing party was sent ashore and returned to report that there was no sign of activity since the previous year. The two vessels then sailed eastwards along Icefjord, but it soon became apparent that they could not penetrate the ice as far as Advent Bay. They turned south towards the entrance to Green Harbour, where Finneset offered a suitable site for a scientific and meteorological station, as an alternative to Quade Hock.

The whole of the fjord, from its junction with Icefjord, was covered with bay ice which Glen reported as up to four feet thick. However, they could see Barentsberg on the eastern slopes, covered with a pall of smoke from the smouldering coal dumps. A long channel would have to be cut through the ice to reach the jetty. This was an arduous job but within the capacity of the ice-breaker *Isbjørn*.

Godfrey, the only experienced and professional soldier in the party, advised immediate action by using relays of sledges to take ashore some arms and supplies. But Sverdrup, mindful of the hard work ahead, preferred a short period of relaxation. In the silence and serenity of that Spitsbergen fjord, surrounded by the mountains, snow and ice of their homeland, there must have been a feeling of relief. Surely the strains and discomforts of their journey would soon be replaced by the achievement of their objective.

It was not until the early hours of the following morning that ice-breaking was resumed. Two reconnaissance parties were sent out, some Norwegians to look around Barentsberg while Glen, Whatman and Sergeant Skribeland went further south along the fjord to investigate Finneset. It was then, at about 05.00 hours on 14 May, that they all saw the first sign of danger. A Ju88 flew along Icefjord at about 600 feet, from Cape Linné towards Advent Bay. It did not turn to investigate, but all the members of the expedition knew that they must have been seen. The reconnaissance parties completed their tasks, finding no sign of activity at either place, but did not get back to the *Isbjørn* until about 17.00 hours. By this time, the ice-breaker had cut a long channel, but there was still much further to go.

Nowadays, Sandy Glen is able to describe the anger of his friend, Dan Godfrey, when Sverdrup refused to accept his advice. Godfrey forecast accurately what could happen after the German aircraft returned to Norway. The two ships, locked in the ice, would be sitting ducks for enemy bombers. But Sverdrup was determined to make straight for the jetty at Barentsberg, through the ice, so that he could unload directly on the shore. Off-loading by sledges would cause delays. He was inflexible and strong-willed, and the commander of the expedition, but his decision was to cost the men dearly.

After 15 hours of ceaseless battering against the ice, the men of the expedition received violent confirmation that their presence had indeed been reported by the Ju88. At 20.30 hours, four Focke-Wulf Kondors suddenly appeared over Green Harbour. In such an enclosed fjord there was no warning of impending attack. On the first two runs at low level, there were near misses as the bombs bounced off the ice before exploding in the air. The Oerlikon fire had no deterrent effect on the four-engined bombers. On the third run, the *Isbjørn* received a direct hit and sank immediately. The aircraft then turned their attention to the *Selis*, which was soon blazing furiously.

Some of the expedition's men were catapulted on to the ice by the force of the explosions. Others who were not part of the gun crews jumped from the ships on to the ice. All survivors were ordered to scatter, to minimise the danger from the machine gun attacks which followed. After it was all over, Glen recounted how his precious pair of spectacles were blown off him by the explosion of one bomb and then returned to him by another; it was a small episode in the eventful career of this extraordinary adventurer.

The attack lasted for about half an hour. With the departure of the last Kondor, silence returned to Green Harbour but the scene had been transformed. Only a hole in the ice marked the sinking of the *Isbjørn*, while the *Selis* was still ablaze. Thirteen men had been killed, including Lieutenant-Colonel Einar Sverdrup and Lieutenant-Colonel Dan Godfrey. Nine men had been wounded, and two of these died. Surprisingly, about 60 men survived unharmed. Nearly all their equipment had been lost: most of their arms and ammunition, food, clothing and wireless – in fact everything that a commander would regard as essential for a successful expedition. The most valuable asset that they retained was their spirit. The survivors were as tough a bunch of men as one could find north of the Arctic Circle.

It was fortunate that Barentsberg was only a few hundred yards away, across the bay ice. In the hurried evacuation of the previous autumn, the accommodation had been left in a condition suitable for reoccupation later. There was adequate shelter, warmth and clothing. A search soon revealed a supply of food, for such settlements usually maintained stocks for the winter. A cache of flour, butter, coffee, tea, sugar and dried mushrooms was soon assembled. There were some sticky sweets for dessert. There was also plenty of frozen pork, for the Arctic provided natural refrigeration for the pigs which had been slaughtered eight months earlier by the Canadians. Tasty omelettes could be made from the eggs of wild duck. There was even a hospital with an adequate supply of dressings for the wounded.

On the day after the attack, there were further visits by Ju88 and

The icebreaker *Isbjørn* breaking a channel through the bay ice at Green Harbour on 14 May 1942.

The icebreaker *Isbjørn* and the sealer *Selis* photographed by Focke Wulf Kondors during the attack on 14 May 1942, while in the channel being cut towards Barentsberg.

(*Far left, top*) Bombs from the Focke Wulf Kondors exploding on and around *Isbjørn* and *Selis*.

(*Far left, bottom*) *Isbjørn* sinking in the ice channel immediately after the attack.

(*Left*) *Selis* left burning and slowly sinking after the attack.

(*Below*) Survivors scatter across the ice after *Isbjørn* has sunk and *Selis* set on fire.

He111 aircraft. The survivors remained well-hidden and there were no further casualties. Mineshafts provided excellent air-raid shelters. Thereafter, there was usually one German aircraft each day, flying eastwards towards Advent Bay or northwards towards Kings Bay. The time interval between departure and return of these aircraft indicated that there might be enemy units in both these fjords.

*

When Leutnant Schütze made his daring departure in the damaged Heinkel on 13 May, he left a dozen men marooned on the airstrip at Bansö, but these were not forgotten by their comrades at Banak. It was a simple matter to route one leg of a weather reconnaissance flight via Icefjord, to drop messages and supplies. It was on one of the first of these flights that Leutnant Bödecker, after turning into Icefjord, on his way to Advent Bay, had been surprised to see the *Isbjørn* cutting a channel towards Barentsberg, with the *Selis* following behind. The German airman knew that the town had been a Russian settlement and had assumed that the two ships were part of a Russian Commando unit. His sighting report had resulted in the prompt attack by the Focke-Wulf Kondors and the destruction of the two vessels.

On the following day, Leutnant Wagner confirmed that the second ship was still burning, and brought back even more important news to Banak. Although the airstrip at Bansö was still too dangerous to use, Dr Etienne had marked out a runway on the bay ice at Advent Bay, where the covering snow was only ten centimetres deep. Wagner had tested the new site, making a successful landing and take-off. This was the good news for which the other pilots had been waiting.

He111s were used to ferry more equipment to Advent Bay, in order to set up a Kröte automatic weather station. They also carried more personnel to supervise its installation. The Kröte itself was taken by Rudolf Schütze, who also carried Regierungsrat Fritz Woelfle, the engineer who had done so much to develop the equipment. Schütze approached Advent Bay by the west coast route, since it was inadvisable to climb over the mountains of the direct route when carrying such a heavy load. He also wanted to take a look at Barentsberg. Here he found the ice channel empty; the second ship had finally sunk. He could see tracks around the buildings, but no sign of any 'Russians'. Moreover, he could see no tracks across the snow between Barentsberg and Longyearbyen. This meant that they could land on the ice without danger from the enemy, and then concentrate their attention on the installation of the Kröte.

Schütze brought his Heinkel down on the same stretch of ice that Wagner had used, and found it as firm as any land runway. However, he noticed that puddles of water formed in his wake, indicating that melting ice might make the landing place unusable before long. A tractor had been provided to tow sledges carrying the heavy equipment to Hjorthamn, where a site had been prepared to set up the Kröte. There was a warm welcome from Dr Etienne and his colleagues, and an excellent meal in comfortable quarters, demonstrating how man's basic needs can be catered for even in very bleak surroundings. There was even a dog, happily wagging its tail.

The automatic weather equipment had been so well constructed that, after transport to Hjorthamn and connection to batteries and aerials, it worked almost immediately. The signals were so clear in Norway that it seemed the Kröte would provide German meteorologists with a service comparable to that of a manned station. Schütze was able to take Woelfle back to Banak on the same day.

Other flights followed, but not with equal success. The puddles which Schütze had noticed were developing into ice-holes which could be highly dangerous for taxying aircraft. On 18 May, Leutnant Bödecker received instructions to pick up Inspector Nieworth, the last member of the four-man winter team to be brought back. Bödecker made a successful landing but, while taxying, his port wheel ran into a weak patch covered with unblemished snow. The wheel suddenly dipped into the water, damaging the undercarriage and a propeller. The Heinkel soon settled lower into the ice-hole and it became apparent that there was no hope of carrying out any repairs.

This was a serious setback to the plans to evacuate all German personnel from Advent Bay. Further flights would have to be deferred for a few days, after the snow had cleared from the airstrip at Bansö. The ground would be too boggy for several days after the thaw but, given suitable weather, it might be expected to dry out sufficiently to permit aircraft to land and then take off when fully laden. Meanwhile the meteorological party, together with the newly-arrived aircrew, had no option but to wait.

The airmen from Banak became rather apprehensive when they

spotted ski tracks in the snow across the Coles Valley. They did not know the size and strength of the potential danger, but could do little more than make harassing flights over Barentsberg and boost morale by dropping mail and essential supplies to their comrades at Bansö.

After the death of Lieutenant-Colonel Sverdrup on 14 May, Lieutenant Ove Roll Lund had assumed command of the Norwegian Forces. It seemed to him that the most immediate danger was the possibility that enemy troops might be despatched to mop up the survivors. To guard against this, he split his forces by sending about 35 men to Sveagruva. This entailed a long and dangerous trek along Grøndalen, across Reindalen, and then over the mountains of Nordenskiöld Land, before descending to the shore of Van Mijen Fjord, off Bell Sound. It was the sort of ordeal that only hardened Arctic veterans could have undertaken successfully. The first men of this party reached their destination after a 36 hour journey, made distressing by the loss of one of their members down a crevasse.

The more able of those who remained at Barentsberg looked after the wounded and kept a low profile when enemy aircraft appeared overhead. However, they also made plans to take aggressive action as soon as relief arrived, and this was something which they expected confidently. The accounts which Sandy Glen subsequently recorded give a clear impression of the spirit with which they overcame their adverse circumstances.

An early objective was to discover the strength of the enemy presence around Advent Bay. This was done by small groups on skis, carrying minimum supplies on their backs, and relying on sheltering in deserted huts en route. For camouflage, they used whatever they could find – Russian bed sheets, pillows and dentists' white coats. They might have looked like armed and marauding Arabs at close quarters, but they hoped not to be noticed from the air against a background of snow.

Two such patrols set out on 16 and 17 May. Their route took them first to Cape Laila, then across the Coles Valley, and finally over the mountains to the mine workings near the junction of Advent Valley and Endalen. The first party included Glen, Whatman and Skribeland. The second included the two best skiers, Sergeant Knutsen and Corporal Ostbye. The two parties joined forces on the fjord slope to the south-east of Longyearbyen, which luckily overlooked the Bansö airstrip. They saw much bustling activity there, as the German weathermen, engineers and airmen concentrated on their equipment. It is probable that the watchers overestimated the strength of the enemy. Some went as far as the Hans Lund Hut but withdrew prudently when they heard the generator working.

Sandy Glen now relates an anecdote about this reconnaissance which demonstrates the verve with which it was carried out. The party saw smoke drifting from the chimney of a small hut which was standing alone. They burst inside to find themselves confronted by a dog instead of the Germans they expected. The reaction of a well-trained Commando would have been to silence the animal immediately, but Glen preferred to treat him in the same way as all his canine friends.

'Hello,' he said, holding out a hand in a friendly gesture. The dog trotted across to be patted, with wagging tail. It raised no objection when the strangers helped themselves to its master's stock of wine. It was not until 37 years later that Glen learned why the dog had been so co-operative. Its German master had named it 'Ullo'.

The ski tracks could not be concealed from the air, particularly across the open stretches of Coles Valley. The expert skiers did their best to confuse the trail by leaving as many criss-crossing tracks as possible. These probably caused the German airmen to overestimate the strength of their opponents. Both reconnaissance parties returned to Barentsberg without loss, having satisfied themselves that the enemy was not strong enough to launch an attack overland. This was a boost for morale, even for those who were wounded and shocked. Confidence grew that a Catalina would arrive eventually. With reinforcements, defence could be turned into attack.

A signal station was set up to prepare for the arrival of the Catalina. The men realised that the aircraft would probably fly along Icefjord, and they chose a site to the north of Barentsberg, at the entrance of Green Harbour not far from Cape Heer. It was manned by Glen, Whatman and Skribeland. Although the hut was far from ideal, the men were warm enough, well fed, and a nearby mine entrance provided shelter against air attack. Whatman and Skribeland managed to make serviceable an Aldis lamp, powered by accumulators and old Russian batteries found in houses in the town. All they could do was wait for help to arrive and to ensure that they did not disclose their position by mistake to an enemy aircraft.

Thus, by the third week of May 1942, there were two small groups occupying makeshift habitations in two fjords running southwards from Icefjord, only ten minutes apart by air. On the ground, however, they were separated by a stretch of inhospitable territory which also protected each from the other.

The Germans hoped to be evacuated. They had the advantages that their parent unit was only 500 miles away and they were in regular communication by radio. Their plight was known, and they were confident that they would be relieved as soon as the landing strip was clear.

The Norwegians had returned to their homeland. They had lost all their military equipment but they were determined to stay. Their nearest help was over 1,000 miles away. They had no means of communication, but their morale was unshaken.

Even if each had known the weakness of the other's position, neither had sufficient strength to mount an attack. The solutions to the problems of both could come only from the air. Both parties were on the alert for the sound of reconnaissance aircraft and the identification of friend or foe.

CHAPTER SIX

Catalina 'P for Peter'

Our new Catalina, serial VA729, bore the letter 'P' on the hull. We should have liked to call it 'P for Polar' but this was debarred on grounds of security. It was thus known as the conventional 'P for Peter'.

It took us just over three hours to fly from the maintenance base at Gourock on the Clyde estuary to Sullom Voe in the Shetlands. This was always a picturesque journey, whether one took the west coast route past the Western Isles and the Minches, or the short cut along the Caledonian Canal between Fort William and Inverness and then northwards along the eastern seaboard of Caithness towards Orkney and the Shetlands. But on this occasion, 21 May 1942, Tim and I were much too concerned about what lay ahead to enthuse about the Scottish scenery. We had to prepare for our polar flights within the next fortnight and there was no one else to whom we could turn for assistance. Ronnie was quiet too, but then he never said much when he concentrated on the job in hand. We had told him of the challenge ahead and he had been quick to catch on to the fact that we would be 'on our own'.

Tim was looking forward to a long talk with our commanding officer, Wing Commander Hutton. In the event, this took a form different from our expectations. He was greeted with the news that Gillie Potier had attacked an He111 on the ground at Advent Bay, one of the potential sites for our advanced base. This meant that the Germans were already at Spitsbergen and that there was the prospect of combat as well as facing the elements. Perhaps the programme would be delayed, or cancelled.

However, the pressure started immediately, as usually happened in squadron life. Instructions arrived the day after we returned to Sullom Voe. They were brief and contained no surprise:

ONE CATALINA TO MAKE RECONNAISSANCE OF SPITSBERGEN TO LOCATE PERSONNEL AND ESTABLISH THEIR NATIONALITY. ROUTE TO BE AS FOLLOWS – SULLOM VOE, SOUTH CAPE,

115

ICEFJORD, CAPE LINNÉ, BARENTSBERG, ADVENT BAY, KINGS FJORD. ON COMPLETION RECONNAISSANCE IS REQUIRED ICE EDGE SOUTH OF SPITSBERGEN TO JAN MAYEN. ALL OPERATIONAL FORMS TO BE RENDERED IN CYPHER 'MOST SECRET'.

This was the full extent of the information given to us. Since fog had obliterated the coastline on our previous flight, we had never seen Spitsbergen, but we made a close examination of the photographs taken by Dick Fairley during Potier's flight and also benefited from his detailed report. We knew that the Fritham expedition should have reached Spitsbergen by 15 May, two days after Potier's flight, and that a wireless signal would have been sent if they had made a successful landing. It seemed from our instructions that no signal had been received and that the primary purpose of our flight was to find out what had happened to them. This might require a search of all the likely fjords along the western coast of Spitsbergen. If that proved inconclusive, we would have to look for the two ships, or survivors, along the edge of the ice pack towards Jan Mayen. It was going to be a long flight.

We know now that the Allied Command was acting on the interception of German wireless signals and their decryption at Bletchley Park. They were aware that the two ships had been attacked and destroyed, but they did not know what had happened to the personnel, because the Germans did not know either. In retrospect, our instructions were phrased brilliantly by the Staff. The inclusion of Barentsberg as the first place to be searched after Cape Linné gave us the correct guidance without disclosing vital information which we might let slip if we were unlucky enough to become PoWs.

We had to spend two days of hectic work in preparing our flying boat for operational work. The additional compasses and other equipment had to be fitted. All was tested and found to be serviceable. Then there was a test flight on 23 May and, after a long night's sleep, we were ready for departure on the morning of 25 May.

The weather forecast was of strong easterly winds to the north of the Shetlands, backing to lighter northerly winds along the ice edge and towards Spitsbergen. This meant that we might be thwarted by fog once more over the reconnaissance area.

The entire crew was on board by 11.00 hours. The men were in their usual happy mood and there were some ribald comments about how to tell the nationality of anyone we might see on the ice.

Scale model of Catalina 'P for Peter', made by Ronald Martin.

'If he stands smartly to attention and salutes, he'll be one of us. If he waves to us, he'll be Norwegian. If he shoots at us, he'll be German. If he has snow on his boots, he'll be Russian.'

Engines were started and moorings slipped at 11.23 hours. We were airborne 15 minutes later and flew on visual courses to North Unst. There was 10/10th low stratus cloud as we set course from the Muckle Flugga lighthouse at a height of 600 feet and with an air temperature of plus 12 degrees Centigrade. Within five minutes, the wind velocity had been established as 9 knots from 135 degrees, and course was altered by five degrees to port, to 042 degrees. We remained on precisely the same compass course for the next eight hours, although the wind direction backed from south-easterly to easterly while the speed varied between 10 and 32 knots, and magnetic variation changed from 13 to 6 degrees west during this time. These alterations meant that the 'track made good' altered by as much as 13 degrees, but on this type of flight we did not make frequent alterations of course to maintain a constant track. We had only to ensure that the changes in wind velocity did not take us too close to enemy-occupied Norway.

We moved from one chart to the next as we flew northwards, and reached the limit of the standard RAF plotting sheets at 71 degrees 30 minutes north. This was presumably the farthest north that the RAF had expected anyone to fly, and at this point we had to change to an Admiralty chart, which was on a different scale.

The cloud base came down lower and we kept beneath it, but we rarely flew below 380 feet. The low cloud was not unwelcome, for it would give cover if we met an enemy aircraft. We were glad to note that the distant-reading compass reconciled perfectly with the other compasses; this was one of the benefits of a new aircraft with a faultless electrical system. It could also be seen that the two special compasses became more stable as we reached the latitudes for which they had been designed.

By 15.11 hours, Tim managed to get a quick sun sight with the marine sextant through thinning cloud. This indicated a position within five miles of dead reckoning. Further sextant sights over three hours later gave less reliable results, for the horizon was hazy, but seemed to indicate that we were approaching too near Bear Island. Eventually, at 19.33 hours, Tim altered course by six degrees to port, to ensure that we did not go too far to the east. The temperature was lower and there were occasional fog patches down to sea level. At 21.22 hours we saw drift ice, indicating that the channel to the north of Bear Island was still unsafe for the Russian convoys.

At 21.46 hours, our radar showed land 35 miles away on our starboard bow, and we altered course towards it. Our original course had been correct after all, and the precautionary alteration had been unnecessary. It was highly satisfactory after ten hours of flying.

By now, the temperature was down to zero, and Tim warned us to watch for aircraft icing. Passing 18 miles from Bear Island, we set course for South Cape of Spitsbergen. To our surprise, the cloud base lifted, improving the prospects of a clear landfall. South Cape came into view at 23.10 hours and I left my navigation table for the blister compartment. For the next two and a half hours, my job would be to take photographs and draft the reconnaissance report, keeping contact with Tim and Ronnie over the intercom. We flew visually along the coastline, past Horn Sound, Isojave and Cape Borthen (where the wreck of a ship with 'USSR' painted on its side had to be photographed) towards Cape Lyell and Cape Linné. The whole of this coastline consisted of precipitous cliffs, flecked with snow and ice, with the tops of the peaks chopped off by a layer of stratus cloud. There were gaps where fjords ran inland to the east. It was an awe-inspiring sight.

As we passed over the deserted radio station at Cape Linné, the broad expanse of Icefjord opened up before us. There was solid bay ice along both sides of the fjord, and it extended into all the minor fjords which branched off to the north and south. Icefjord itself, which is over ten miles wide towards the entrance, gave an impression of such immensity that our Catalina seemed no more than a little bird of passage, alone in the frozen north. There was a lead of black open water down the centre of the fjord, but it was flanked by large floes of drift ice, which seemed stationary when viewed from above. It was evident that we would be unable to land there. Ronnie Martin remembers his first sight of Spitsbergen:

Before we entered Icefjord, Tim had warned all the crew to keep a sharp lookout for enemy aircraft. We were flying at about 700 feet and fortunately the cloud was 10/10th with the base down to 1,500 feet, so that this gave us somewhere to hide if anything came along. It was around midnight, with the sun only just above the horizon, and Spitsbergen gave the impression of a very forbidding place in this poor light. The sides of the flat-topped mountains looked as though they had been scored vertically by a huge rake. The lower parts were covered with snow, but the upper parts were freer as a result of melting or wind. We flew on up Icefjord towards Advent Bay, with Tim on manual controls, and turned in there.

It took half an hour to reach Advent Bay and Longyearbyen. This was no more than a group of scattered houses nestling at the foot of the steep slopes on the western side of Advent Valley. We saw pylons and overhead conveyor lines leading from the mines on the hill slopes towards the frozen jetty. There were more pylons across the floor of the valley, some toppled over on their sides. So far, we had seen no sign of life – no smoke, no movement, only a vast expanse of white desolation. Then, suddenly, we saw the wreckage of an He111, in a hole in the ice not far from the jetty. The main part of the fuselage and the engines were lying in the water. The aircraft was supported only by the wing tips and the tailplane, which were resting on the ice around the edge of the waterhole.

Naturally, we jumped to the conclusion that this was the Heinkel that Potier had shot up a fortnight earlier. In fact, the position of this had been on the landing strip about three miles further along the valley. We cruised around the area, but saw no signs of any other activity. Photographs were taken from various angles, for later examination.

So far, we had seen no trace of the Fritham expedition. The Heinkel confirmed that the enemy had been there, and might still be hiding in the township. Our next orders were to search the coastline further to the north, before heading towards Jan Mayen, and we turned and made our way westwards along the southern shoreline of Icefjord. Ronnie Martin continues:

We saw no sign of life in the buildings around Longyearbyen, although there were a few ski marks. I did the flying on the way back to Green Harbour, while the lookouts in the blisters used binoculars. They had a wider field of vision than the pilots, and they could also stand up and sweep around more easily than in the cockpit. When we were near the entrance of Green Harbour, one of the blister lookouts said there was smoke coming up. Of course, we knew that the coal dumps had been set on fire by the Canadian expedition during the previous autumn and that was probably the reason. Nevertheless, Tim decided to take a closer look and took over the controls.

The solid mass of bay ice extended from the edge of Icefjord all the

Heinkel 111 damaged while taxying across the bay ice at Advent Bay on 18 May 1942.

Another view of the same He111.

The Heinkel 111 in the ice hole, photographed by Catalina 'P for Peter' at 01.00 hours on 26 May 1942.

The two wireless aerials of the *Kröte* weather station at Hjorthamn in Advent Bay, with the He111 abandoned in the ice hole, just discernible between them.

way into the side fjord but, as soon as we turned into this, it became apparent that the expedition had been there before us. A long and straight channel had been cut through the ice towards the settlement. The channel ended with a circle of clear water, a few hundred yards from the shore. It looked as though an elongated keyhole had been carved out of the ice, and it could have been done only by an ice-breaker. The circle at the end might have been made so that the vessel could turn and make its way out again, but it might have had more serious implications.

There were more pylons along the slopes of the fjord, as well as a frozen jetty and some installations down at the shore line. The smoke was rising from the smouldering coal dumps. There were tracks in the snow between some of the buildings, but no sign of any movement. Ronnie Martin remarks:

> I have sometimes wondered why we did not spot the 'keyhole' effect in the ice on our starboard side when we passed the entrance of Green Harbour an hour before. It might have been because the ice had partially broken up in the eleven days since the ships had been bombed and sunk. Icefjord was littered with drift ice, so that perhaps the hole was less obvious until we were nearer to it. However, just after we saw the hole, one of the blister lookouts reported a flashing light directed at us from one of the huts.

At the time, I was fully occupied taking photographs of the township and the cutting in the ice. Then Tim turned towards the hut, where two men were waving to us as well as flashing with an Aldis lamp. One of the two men looked like Sandy Glen. A photograph was taken to make sure.

The message flashed to us read:

FRITHAM SHIPS SUNK NOTHING SAVED SURVIVORS HERE GERMANS IN ADVENT BAY IS DAILY RECCO IN FORCE HELP ESSENTIAL

Tim replied by Aldis lamp:

RECCO WHEN WEATHER OK WILL ORGANISE HELP GOD BLESS TIM HEALY

Back came a further message:

SOME SURVIVORS SV. . .R. . . AND WOUNDED HERE

It was difficult to read such messages when circling in a Catalina. There was no position from which one person could read the whole message, since wings, nose and tail unit always blocked the line of sight at some time. Our procedure for overcoming the problem was to appoint a main reader, the navigator or maybe a wireless operator, to stand between the blister cupolas and read out the letters as they were received. If he missed a letter, someone else would intervene and continue until the main reader could take over again. The pilots received a steady flow of letters over the intercom and intervened with complete words as the gist of the message became apparent. But sometimes a sudden movement of the aircraft caused part of the message to be missed by everyone. Tim thought that SV. . .R. . was either SVALBARD or SVERDRUP, but it was probably the township of SVEAGRUVA. It was described as a confused message in the intelligence report.

We had been over Icefjord for over an hour and for half that time our tight manoeuvres had been using up valuable fuel. We could delay no longer if we were to achieve the second part of our reconnaissance, an examination of the southern edge of the ice pack. Our beleaguered friends were left in their stark surroundings and, at 01.45 hours, we set course from Cape Linné towards Jan Mayen Island.

At first, it was very pleasant, flying across the ice-free waters of Spitsbergen Bay. The cloud was still 10/10th stratus with a base of 1,400 feet, the wind was light and the temperature above zero. The aircraft was steady in the calm air and it was an excellent opportunity to have a hot meal and start preparing the reconnaissance report. Then everyone on board could settle down to the next long leg of the journey.

Drift ice was again sighted when we reached the western edge of the bay, at 04.20 hours. An hour later, the sea ice became more solid and the aircraft was enveloped in fog. The temperature dropped to below zero, and everyone was looking for the first signs of aircraft icing. This began at 06.09 hours, when the astro compass mountings began to look like small Christmas trees. Within a couple of minutes, the ice was two inches thick on projecting items. Ronnie Martin recalls:

This was the worst icing-up we experienced on all our flights. Tim

Cape Heer, at the entrance to Green Harbour, photographed from 'P for Peter' on 26 May 1942. It shows smoke over Barentsberg, bay ice in Green Harbour and drift ice in Icefjord.

Lieutenant-Commander A.R. Glen and Major A.B. Whatman waving to 'P for Peter', from a hut near Barentsberg. The two men were among the survivors of the sunken vessels *Isbjørn* and *Selis*.

decided to turn around to get out of the freezing fog, and asked the engineer for auto-rich because our indicated airspeed was dropping. He controlled the turn knob of George while I controlled the height knob. We were flying at about 300 feet and could just see the drift ice below us, looking for all the world like giant crazy paving – not the place to have to make a forced landing. The air in the cockpit became intensely cold. Perhaps this was not only the effect of the freezing fog outside but the result of a touch of fear within.

I switched on the de-icing equipment. The rubber 'boots' extended almost the whole length of the leading edges of the main wing, rudder and tailplane. They pulsated and cracked off lumps of ice, some of which made quite a frightening noise as they flashed past and hit the hull of the aircraft. The de-icing fluid sprayed on to the propeller blades so that ice was flung off, striking the hull at specially reinforced points.

Tim continued turning the aircraft, trying to find some clear air free from ice, and after about 30 minutes we left the drift ice behind as well as the freezing fog.

It was certainly a great relief to find that this equipment did its work perfectly, and to see the fuselage and struts reassume their normal shapes. With 33 inches boost and maximum engine revolutions, the Catalina had been staggering along at only 85 knots. But by 06.40 hours, the drift ice below had been replaced by brash ice, and we were soon over clear water again.

After that experience, it seemed too dangerous to try to reach Jan Mayen. It was better to return to Sullom Voe, to be ready for another sortie to Barentsberg with a minimum of delay. We turned towards the Shetlands.

By 11.25 hours, we were back in the same air stream that we had experienced on the outward journey. The dead reckoning navigation proved to be accurate and we were waterborne at 14.27 hours, mooring up seven minutes later.

The engines had been working non-stop for 27 hours 10 minutes. So had we. But there was still much to be done before we could go to bed. A detailed record of the position of the ice edge had to be prepared, specifying the types of ice and the heights at which we had been flying. Intelligence reports, photographic summaries and all the customary action at the end of a reconnaissance sortie had to be completed. There was only one variation. For security reasons, my navigation log was not handed in for analysis.

The fate of the expedition had been established. The position of the ice edge between Bear Island and Spitsbergen had been reported, as well as the ice edge to about 150 miles east of Jan Mayen. We had carried out the objectives contained in our orders.

The survivors at Barentsberg needed help urgently, and the only way to provide it was by air lift. There was no possibility of a landing until one of the fjords was clear of ice. A parachute drop from a Catalina was not practicable. The best solution was to pack supplies into small containers which could be thrown from the blister cupolas while flying as low as possible along the lower slopes at the side of the fjord. We would have to look for some deep snow drifts and hope that a cushioned impact, followed by rolling down the slope, might prevent the containers from bursting. Preference would have to be given to sturdy supplies that would not break easily. Long streamers, with orange cloth knotted at intervals like a kite, would help the survivors to find the containers in deep snow.

A major difficulty was that the Catalina was already heavily laden with extra fuel to give us the required range. The total weight of extra supplies that we could carry was severely limited. The first step was to remove from the aircraft all items of equipment that we could dispense with. The nine crew parachutes, personal kit, bunk fittings, flares and even sea markers were taken out. The aircraft was stripped of all but absolute essentials.

All this work was organised with great gusto by our flight commander, Squadron Leader H.B. Johnson, and his enthusiastic staff. They put themselves into the shoes of the survivors to decide what their most urgent needs might be. Since Spitsbergen was a natural refrigerator, it seemed reasonable to assume that Barentsberg would have yielded some supplies of frozen food. It was decided that the men would prefer medical supplies and warm clothing, together with minor luxuries to improve morale, such as cigarettes, tobacco, jam, chocolate, tinned meat and such like.

There was no time to collect supplies from the mainland. Everything had to come from the NAAFI and the resources of Sullom Voe. The survivors would be unlikely to complain if they received RAF blue battledress, long johns, flying suits and gloves. Someone remarked that, if a land battle developed, the enemy would be surprised to find themselves faced with a force that looked like the RAF Regiment.

The prevalence of fog around Spitsbergen and the difficulty of finding the precise location of the survivors in poor visibility meant that Tim Healy and his crew and our 'P for Peter' were probably the best to act as carriers. Our most urgent need was for sleep, and we left the organisation to others and went to bed. In the top drawer of my desk was a schedule of all the work that still had to be done in preparation for the flight to the North Pole. This was no longer an urgent priority and could be locked away.

For this next flight, and some subsequent ones, authorisations from Headquarters were given by telephone, largely to approve the actions taken on local initiative. Kit bags and parachute bags were used as containers. In addition to the supplies we had already gathered, we included a Tommy gun, ten pans of ammunition, a Very Light pistol with two dozen red and white cartridges, and a simple signalling code for later flights.

Once all these supplies were on board, the laden weight of the aircraft was considerably above the safe limit, and Ronnie had to be very painstaking about weight distribution. Final adjustments delayed our departure until the late afternoon of 28 May. This was unfortunate, for it meant that we might not reach Barentsberg until after dawn. The dropping runs and exchange of messages would probably take an hour, so there was the possibility that we might meet an enemy aircraft on its morning reconnaissance. We would just have to be alert.

Just before we left the Operations Room, we received a confidential message from our friends in the officers' mess. They had decided that the best uplift to the morale of a beleaguered naval officer was the present of a bottle of rum. With great care, the incandescent part of a flare had been removed and replaced with a bottle of this warming spirit. The contraption had been reassembled and fitted in the flare chute. All Tim had to do was to pull the handle at the right moment and the bottle would float down attached to a small parachute, accompanied by a message of good cheer to Sandy from all his friends at Sullom Voe.

The weather forecast was good for our safety but not for ease of flying. Sullom Voe was covered with 10/10th stratus cloud at 300 feet, and this was likely to extend far northwards. Once again, it would have to be a low-level flight all the way. The wind was likely to be from the east at first, backing towards northerly and increasing in speed as we flew northward. Thus, the ground speed might drop below 60 knots towards Spitsbergen, so that the outward journey could take over 13 hours. However, Icefjord should be on the leeward side of the mountains, giving good prospects of clear visibility over Barentsberg.

Engines were started and moorings slipped at 16.32 hours. Ronnie Martin remembers the problems of take-off:

Unfortunately, the easterly wind meant that the run was towards some hills at the end of Garth Voe. All the other wind directions gave runs towards fairly open water. So after the usual warming-up and testing procedures, Tim edged the Catalina as near the down-wind shore as he dared. He opened up the throttles and, as usual, I held them open.

The aircraft took much longer than normal to climb on to the step and then Tim signalled 'floats up' to help reduce drag. All the time the shoreline was approaching rapidly. We were still on the water even after our normal lift-off speed had been reached, but Tim did not want to pull the Catalina off the water too soon in case it dropped back again.

We were not far off the shore when Tim eased back on the control column and we literally climbed up the grassy slopes, with grazing sheep scattering in all directions. We cleared the hills with a few feet to spare and Tim throttled back a little and levelled off just below the cloud base and set course northwards.

I believe that some of the personnel in the operations room which overlooked the Voe were taking bets as to whether we would get off. So someone lost some money there.

Tim tried to coast-crawl to North Unst but this was invisible even from 300 feet. We set course from a dead-reckoning position, confirmed by a radar bearing. An hour later, we were down to 200 feet in continous rain, sometimes dropping to 100 feet to be in visual contact with the sea. Regular drift-taking was essential, as our only method of dead-reckoning navigation for twelve hours, in such conditions.

During the first four hours, our only sightings were of floating mines and an empty life raft. By the end of this period, the wind had dropped to below 10 knots and there were fog patches down to the sea in places. The cloud became even thicker after another hour. As forecast, the wind backed and increased in strength, to 48 knots. Our ground speed dropped to 58 knots, while the temperature approached zero. To avoid icing up, we had to keep altering course around the thickest patches of fog.

Then visibility began to improve. By 03.21 hours, the wind had veered and dropped to 14 knots. The cloud base lifted and the horizon became clear. The first floes of drift ice came into view about 40 minutes later. At 04.19 hours, the radar showed land ahead at a range of 55 miles. Soon we were flying visually along the west coast of Spitsbergen, and then round the corner from Icefjord to Green Harbour. For over twelve and a half hours we had never flown above 380 feet, and for much of the time we had been below 150 feet. It was the sort of flying which imposed a great strain on all on board, especially the pilots.

Arrival at the dropping zone brought a feeling of relief as well as a bustling activity. The pilots could fly and manoeuvre manually. The flight engineers made frequent switches to rich mixture. I was busy with photography and reading Aldis messages. Others were engaged on throwing out packages, in a disciplined sequence. The bags were held outside the blisters in a 100 knot slipstream and dropped as we approached the huts at the foot of the hill slope. We were all intensely busy while the Catalina was making steep turns inside the fjord, and at the same time had to keep a sharp lookout for any enemy aircraft approaching from Icefjord.

There was still too much drift ice in the fjords to attempt a landing, and messages were passed by Aldis lamp.

IF I AM ABLE TO LAND SHALL I BE SAFE FROM ENEMY ACTION?
YES
CAN YOU ESTIMATE ENEMY STRENGTH?
40
ARE YOU IN IMMEDIATE NEED OF ARMS AND AMMUNITION?
YES
WHAT ARE YOUR NUMBERS?
30
HOW MANY WOUNDED?
6
ARE YOU IN IMMEDIATE DANGER FROM ENEMY IN LOCALITY?
YES
IS ENEMY DOING AIR RECCO?
YES EVERY DAY FOUR CONDORS 03.00 TO 04.00
DO YOU NEED ADDITIONAL FOOD?
NO

There was some delay in the reply to these questions and some, such as 'Do you need additional clothes?', 'Have you a doctor?', and 'When is the best time to land on future sorties?', were not answered at all. We learnt afterwards the reason for the delay and confusion. A German aircraft had flown out of Icefjord and was above the clouds while we were creeping in underneath. The ground party had been listening to both sets of engines and trying to distinguish between them. This episode was typical of the war in the Arctic.

We had spent an hour over Barentsberg and could linger no longer. Tim waggled the wings of 'P for Peter' in farewell, and we returned to Cape Linné to begin our homeward journey. That was at 06.40 hours. Again, we were at 300 feet, but the temperature was above freezing.

After our spirits had been lifted by a hot meal and some tea, I went up front to ask if the rum had been delivered safely. Tim looked at Ronnie, in silence. They both looked at the flare handle. It had not been pulled, in the excitement and concentration of the occasion.

'Don't look,' said Tim, and pulled the handle. The blister gun watch did not comment. We agreed that we could not ruin the enthusiasm of those at base by admitting that we had forgotten.

The return journey was a replica of the outward flight, but in reverse order. There were light winds at first, then strong winds from the north-east which pushed up our ground speed to 147 knots. Then there were light winds again and poor visibility. By 11.30 hours we were just under the cloud base and it was raining heavily. We managed to obtain some wireless bearings from Norwegian stations and these reconciled with the navigation plot. At 16.17 hours Sullom Voe beacon appeared on the radar screen straight ahead, a rectangular blob at a range of 64 miles.

We were waterborne at 17.00 hours, and safely moored up 10 minutes later. The return journey had taken just over ten hours and we had been in the air for 24 hours 38 minutes. We had completed 51 hours of flying in just over four days and were required to make another delivery run the morning after the next. Meanwhile, the supplies had been delivered, and no questions were asked about the rum. Very little time was spent on reports, messages being passed to Headquarters by telephone. Our main interest was in food and sleep.

The next load of supplies had to include arms and ammunition. Tim hoped that, if ice conditions continued to improve, he might be able to put the Catalina down in a clear stretch of water and then taxi towards the shore. If so, it would be possible to deliver a wireless, better medical supplies, and perhaps evacuate the wounded.

After two nights of refreshing sleep, we were ready to tackle another delivery run to Spitsbergen. Unfortunately, take-off had to be delayed until the evening. This meant that we would be flying after a full day of activity and that we would reach Barentsberg around mid-day. At this time it would be easier to find a clear stretch for landing, but it might bring us into contact with patrolling enemy aircraft. The weather forecast was also unfavourable. Some heavy storms had passed over the Shetlands during the past two days, and we would catch up with these on our way northward.

Moorings were slipped at 23.17 hours on 31 May and we were airborne in 'P for Peter' 13 minutes later. As usual we set course from North Unst, at a height of 450 feet and with an air temperature of plus nine degrees Centigrade. There was a light westerly wind at first, but this soon backed and strengthened. After a short while we noticed a discrepancy of five degrees between the distant-reading and the P4 compasses. We had to decide which to use and to keep a note of a possible error in dead-reckoning.

At about 02.30 hours the sea had become flat calm and the wind had slackened, but it was raining from a cloud base of 600 feet. As yet, there was no danger from icing. After 05.50 hours the weather started to improve, but two hours later the wind backed and strengthened once more. Tim managed to get two quick sun sights which indicated that we were close to our plotted position. But such were the vagaries of Arctic weather that within ten minutes a heavy bank of stratus cloud stretched ahead of us, covering the entire horizon. We could not avoid it and, by 07.49 hours were flying through a snow storm.

Icing began at 08.40 hours and it built up very quickly. By then, we were about 200 miles away from Bear Island and we knew that these conditions would last all the way to Spitsbergen. There was only one prudent course of action, to abandon the delivery flight. At 08.54 hours, we turned back to base.

There was a welcome rise in the temperature as we flew southwards. We were under 10/10th cloud for a long time, and we stayed as low as 200 feet to keep within sight of the waves. The wind dropped and then increased again. I managed to get a rather hazy sun sight at 14.30 hours, and adjusted our dead-reckoning position accordingly. We had been flying out of sight of land for 15 hours. By

15.41 hours it was raining heavily but the cloud base had lifted sufficiently for us to climb to 1,000 feet. We sighted the Shetlands on our port bow at 16.34 hours and landed half an hour later. The ground crews were not expecting us, for we had not broken W/T silence, and mooring-up was delayed for 35 minutes.

Although this sortie had been shorter than the others, just over 18 hours, it had been much more tiring. The late start and poor weather conditions had added to the strain. We had missed three nights' sleep in a week and had worked on three occasions for over 30 hours at a stretch. On all three flights there had been periods of 10 to 17 hours between landfalls. My three sets of navigation logs recorded over 200 drift measurements and 180 calculations of wind velocity. For most of the time, we had flown below 600 feet. Although we were all young and fit, all nine of us were utterly exhausted when we clambered into the dinghy.

A longer period of rest was required before we could continue our contribution to Operation Fritham. For us, the storms which passed over Sullom Voe during the next few days proved a blessing in disguise.

CHAPTER SEVEN

Turning Point

After we made our flight over Spitsbergen on 26 May 1942, the Germans in Bansö reported our reconnaissance to their headquarters at Banak in Norway. Nevertheless, the Luftwaffe was not too concerned about the men at Advent Bay, for we had not penetrated far enough to the south to discover their presence in the Hans Lund Hut. The Germans could only wait and hope that more encouraging news would soon arrive. This was transmitted from Bansö on 12 June, four weeks after the two Norwegian ships were bombed at Barentsberg. The message read:

GROUND DRYING QUICKLY. POSSIBILITY OF LANDING, PROBABLY FROM 14 JUNE.

Leutnant Wagner was the first to make the attempt, in a Ju88. The ground was indeed dry enough for a landing, but the Arctic had other dangers in store. These were summarised in the next message:

JU88 LANDED SMOOTHLY. ON TAXYING PROPELLERS DAMAGED. TWO COMPLETE PROPELLERS NEEDED.

Thus, there were now 18 Germans marooned at Bansö, consisting of two complete aircrews as well as the meteorologists. Flights were made daily over them, in the hope that conditions would improve, but each aircraft received a red Very signal. At last, on 25 June, spirits were lifted by a more optimistic message:

FROM TOMORROW POSSIBILITY OF LANDING FOR HE111 AND JU52.

This time it was the turn of Rudolf Schütze, who took off at 01.00 hours the following day. But when he arrived over Longyearbyen a few hours later, there was another red signal. Back he went to Banak, disappointed once more. The Arctic was not yet ready for them.

The Germans even considered using floatplanes to carry out the evacuation, but the eastern end of Icefjord and the whole of Advent Bay were still littered with floes of drift ice which would have ripped the floats to shreds. Further to the west, along the coast of Spitsbergen and the entrances to Icefjord and Green Harbour, the bay ice was steadily disappearing as the summer solstice approached. This gave the Germans some cause for worry, for there was the possibility that another Allied seaborne force might arrive.

The Allied officers at Barentsberg had also been monitoring the progress of the spring thaw, with enthusiasm. Although they had few resources and were unable to communicate directly with headquarters, the prospects of relief improved steadily. They hoped that, on its next flight, the Catalina might be able to land and taxi to the shore. This could prove a turning point in their fortunes. The wounded could be evacuated, the reports that Lund and Glen had carefully prepared could be taken back to London, and plans for reinforcement set in motion. Morale at Barentsberg had been put under strain by the frequent bombing by the German aircraft from Banak, but the receding ice brought a revival of confidence. In particular, Sandy Glen believed implicitly that Tim Healy would come to their support.

Meanwhile, the British Admiralty responded, as one might expect, in accordance with the reports they received. When they learnt of the fate of Operation Fritham after our flight of 26 May, plans for reinforcement were altered to a rescue operation. Then our second report arrived, three days later, indicating that the plight of the survivors was not so serious as was first thought. The matter could be reconsidered once more.

The Admiralty made generous expressions of appreciation of the contribution from Coastal Command. The Director of the Naval Intelligence Division, Rear Admiral John H. Godfrey, asked Air Marshal Sir Philip Joubert to pass on his thanks to the captain and navigator of the Catalina and their aircrew. This message was passed down through each step in the chain of command, receiving additional comments en route. It was interesting for me to learn of my apparent elevation in status, embodied by the reference to 'their' aircrew, for normally references were made to the captain and 'his' aircrew. This was accentuated by Rear Admiral Godfrey's comment: 'The difficulties of navigation in such latitudes are very apparent to me as a Navigating Officer. . . .' Nevertheless, we in 'P for Peter' did not regard navigation in high latitudes as more than an extension of normal dead-reckoning. It required greater care and precision, as well as more physical endurance. While we could be reasonably proud of our achievements, we all regarded ourselves as under the leadership of one person, Tim Healy.

Another signal, from HQ Coastal Command to Sullom Voe on 4 June, was more interesting. This advised the ground support team for the attempt to fly to the North Pole that they were released from standby. These men had been assembled at Invergordon for embarkation on the *Quest*, which was destined for Spitsbergen. Thus, the HQ staff had evidently decided that the polar attempt was in abeyance, at least for the time being. Nevertheless, Tim did not allow the signal to affect our own preparations. 'Press on,' he commented. 'When the opportunity comes, we might get very short notice.'

At Sullom Voe, we were ready for the next relief flight to Spitsbergen by 5 June. The delivery load consisted mainly of armaments, 24 Ross rifles strapped together with alternating butts to barrels, in bundles of six and four, together with 3,000 rounds of ammunition. There were also general supplies, medical supplies and, equally important, messages for the beleaguered party.

Unfortunately, the storms in the previous week had left the sea too rough for take-off by our heavily-laden flying boat. Departure was delayed until the morning of 6 June. The weather was still unpleasant, with cloud clinging to the hills at only 200 feet, and patches of mist and fog down to sea level in places. By contrast, the forecast for the northerly journey was good. A large anticyclone was expected to cover the whole area. Winds were forecast as light and variable, with the probability of mist and fog in patches along the Spitsbergen coastline.

We slipped moorings at 07.05 hours and were airborne 16 minutes later. Land disappeared immediately after take-off but Tim was prepared for this and our Catalina was soon over the open water of St Magnus Bay to the west of the Shetlands. He did not like setting course from an estimated position but on this occasion there was no option, even from a height of 140 feet.

An hour later, we were still flying at less than 200 feet, but the wind had increased to 26 knots from the south-east and visibility was improving. By 09.15 hours, the cloud base had lifted to 800 feet and visibility had improved to about 30 miles, which was most unusual on our Arctic flights. The horizon cleared and we managed to take some snap sun sights.

As we approached the centre of the anticyclone, the sea became

Western coastline of Spitsbergen between Horn Sound and Icefjord, with peaks covered by stratus cloud, as Catalina 'P for Peter' approached on 6 June 1942.

Landfall at Horn Sound, with peaks covered by stratus cloud, and with 1/10th drift ice, on 6 June 1942

flat calm, the drift negligible, and the wind no more than five knots from an easterly direction. At 11.21 hours, while flying at 100 feet, we saw an aircraft on the eastern horizon. It was probably a Heinkel, but at this stage of the flight Tim was not feeling bellicose. Instead, we found cloud cover at 1,800 feet and avoided further contact. Twenty minutes later, we were down again at 600 feet, flying safely in clear air. By 15.00 hours, we were passing into the northerly section of the anticyclone, where the wind turned to south-easterly and increased in strength.

As forecast, mist and fog patches developed as we approached Spitsbergen. We sighted land far away on the starboard bow at 16.35 hours, and the beam aerials of the radar picked it up 20 minutes later. It was reassuring after flying over an apparently limitless expanse of ocean for ten hours. By 17.01 hours, Ronnie Martin recognised the distinctive features of Horn Sound, and the two pilots coast-crawled northwards to Cape Linné.

The entrance to Icefjord was fog-bound, made worse by a snow flurry. Tim circled for ten minutes until the snow cleared, and then edged his way round the corner to Green Harbour, flying near the shore and just above the water. It was the sort of manoeuvre that could be carried out only by a pilot who knew the fjord and was determined to reach his objective.

Inside Green Harbour a southerly wind was blowing along the length of the fjord, bringing clearer visibility. There had been only a few scattered floes of ice along the coastline, while the centre of Icefjord was clear. A steady flow of brash and drift ice was moving northwards along the edges of Green Harbour, escaping towards the sea along the southern edge of Icefjord. Beyond Barentsberg, the southern part of Green Harbour was still covered by solid bay ice, but there was clear water in the centre, near the entrance.

Signals from the ground party confirmed that there were no enemy aircraft in the vicinity. Tim dropped a message giving a list of the supplies to be dropped, stating that we intended to land, and asking that the wounded be prepared for evacuation. The arms and packages were quickly thrown out, and we learnt later that the rifles suffered little harm from their rough treatment.

Tim returned to the open water at the entrance to Green Harbour. Ronnie Martin remembers the events:

Tim circled around to pick his line of approach, for there were still a few small ice floes moving towards the main fjord. He straightened up into what wind there was, and started to lose height. As we dropped below 100 feet, he was concentrating so much on the surface of the water that he had not signalled 'floats down'. I asked him if he was actually going to land and he nodded, so I signalled Sergeant Baird to lower the floats. Tim made a perfect landing.

As Tim taxied towards the shore, Sergeant Campbell climbed out of the front turret and stood on the small step on the port side of the nose. He took the anchor out of its locker; this was attached to a steel cable leading up from the keel. I stood on the step on the starboard side and plumbed the depth of the water with a lead line, signalling to Tim with my fingers: four fathoms . . . three fathoms. When it was down to two fathoms, Tim stopped the engines and Sergeant Campbell dropped the anchor. It held first time.

Twenty minutes after landing, we were exchanging Aldis and semaphore signals with the ground party. It was no easy matter to launch the dinghy through the port blister cupola, for we dared not remove the Browning .50 machine gun. Stepping down into it required even greater dexterity. Only two men paddled to the shore.

Flight Lieutenant Healy and Sergeant Thomas paddling ashore in the collapsible dinghy from Catalina 'P for Peter', at Green Harbour on 6 June 1942. The photograph is badly marked in places.

Tim took Sergeant Thomas with him, partly because he was very strong and reliable, and partly to ensure that, if they ran into trouble, those remaining on board were capable of returning home without them. They carried ashore a Lewis machine gun, together with a stand and magazines, as well as an Aldis lamp and battery, another Very pistol and cartridges, and a sheaf of messages.

The light and bull-nosed craft proved very difficult to handle against a cross-wind, and they steered a very erratic course. A slight change of wind brought some ice floes to hamper their progress. These were just difficulties that they were determined to overcome, cheered on from the shore by Lund, Glen, Whatman and several others who had gathered to welcome them.

We who remained on board were on strict alert. Ronnie Martin assumed command, and can remember the occasion clearly:

My instructions from Tim were to take off at the first sign of an aircraft or a ship of any sort. Then I was to leave the area as quickly as possible and try to reach some clouds in which to hide. I would then have to watch the fuel situation and return to base if necessary, and come back on another day to pick them up. The

Pilot Officer R. Martin and Sergeant J.E. Campbell fending ice floes from the bow of 'P for Peter' after landing in Green Harbour, near Barentsberg, on 6 June 1942.

Cape Heer, showing the entrance to Green Harbour free of ice, on 14 June 1942.

Landfall at Cape Borthen in Catalina 'P for Peter' on 14 June 1942. There is 7/10th drift ice, with brash ice near the coast.

Cape Linné, at the entrance to Icefjord, on 14 June 1942.

hours we were still flying at 140 feet, although the cloud base was 2,000 feet. At this stage we were to the south-west of Bear Island, and wished to keep below any radar that the Germans might have installed there.

We switched on the radar at 18.11 hours, using the homing aerials, and carried out our standard procedure of a flat turn to 60 degrees on either side of the aircraft heading, to search for our intended landfall. A blip duly appeared on our port bow at a range of 50 miles, and we altered course towards it, then easing our way northwards round the coast with the help of the radar. Visibility decreased as we set course for Spitsbergen. The first sighting of drift ice was about 40 miles to the north of Bear Island, which should please the Admiralty, but they would not welcome the sightings of scattered floes all the way to Spitsbergen on our final leg. The channel was not yet clear for the convoy to North Russia.

Spitsbergen was soon picked up on the radar screen. As we approached the coastline the wind veered and increased to 30 knots. As we passed the entrance to Horn Sound, the katabatic wind swept down the slopes from high glaciers, funnelled by the sides of the fjord to a speed of 48 knots. This churned up the surface of the sea, 350 feet beneath us, and increased our drift from 11 to 25 degrees.

By 21.03 hours, we were circling over Barentsberg. There was no response from the signal station, but some men were waving to us from a hut about half a mile north of the town. This was about 400 feet above sea level, near a mine shaft, and we learnt later that it was their new home since it was safer from air attacks. It did not take long to exchange recognition signals, drop supplies, and pass a message on to Sandy Glen about our intention to land and take him back to Britain for consultations.

On this occasion the northern part of the fjord was completely clear of ice, and by 21.55 hours we had landed and were taxying back towards the town. The steep sides of the fjord gave welcome shelter from the east wind, and it was unnecessary to drop anchor. We merely lay offshore with engines gently ticking over. Eventually, an exuberant Sandy Glen came out in a skiff, accompanied by two Norwegian colleagues, Lieutenant Ross and Private Lingen. We had already spent nearly an hour on the water and, as soon as the three passengers were aboard, Tim lost no time in taxying out to the open water and taking off.

Our next task was to check the position of the ice edge to the west of Spitsbergen. Course was set for position 74 degrees North 05

Lieutenant-Commander Glen (left) wearing RAF uniform, with Flight Lieutenant Healy, at Sullom Voe at 14.00 hours on 16 June 1942.

(*Left*) Lieutenant-Commander Glen on arrival at Sullom Voe, at 06.00 hours on 16 June 1942. (*Right*) Wing Commander H.B. Johnson, DFC, who commanded 210 Squadron from June 1942 to January 1943.

degrees East, in accordance with orders. The wind blew from the north-west at less than 10 knots. The sea was calm, with the customary fog patches down to the surface, but there was no danger of icing since the temperature was plus 13 degrees Centigrade.

Around midnight, we seemed to be passing through frontal conditions, but a couple of hours later we were back in calmer air, with more fog but no icing. At 03.30 hours the expected wireless message arrived:

WEATHER AT BASE: CLOUD BASE 2,500; VIS 20; WIND LIGHT VARIABLE. AKUREYRI: CLOUD BASE 800; VIS 20; WIND NORTH 10. REYKJAVIK FIT.

This indicated that there was no need for us to change our schedule. Shortly afterwards, the radar picked up the mountains of Jan Mayen Island at a range of 88 miles, even though we were flying at only 500 feet. Decreasing visibility indicated that we were approaching sea ice. Scattered floes appeared, the first since leaving Spitsbergen, when we were still 25 miles from the island. The fog thickened so that, when the radar picked up Young's Foreland at the north-east corner of the island, we skirted round to the south and headed to our next turning point at 68 degrees North 18 degrees West. Clearly, there was no navigable channel for a convoy to the north of Jan Mayen Island.

Then the weather deteriorated very rapidly, fog being replaced by heavy rain. The temperature dropped to zero, bring the danger of icing. It was dangerous to continue the reconnaissance to the south-west of Jan Mayen and, at 06.31 hours, we set course for Iceland. We made a landfall to the east of Eyja Fjord and 'P for Peter' was eventually waterborne at Akureyri at 09.30 hours. Another 25 hour flight had been completed, with all objectives substantially achieved.

The Admiralty needed the results of our ice reconnaissance urgently, but security considerations made long wireless signals inadvisable. Thus we took off just before midnight on the same day, for the six-hour transit flight to Sullom Voe. Arriving there safely, Sandy and Tim made long telephone reports to London, and arrangements were put into hand for personal visits on the following day. We went as passengers in a Catalina leaving at 04.15 hours for Woodhaven on the Firth of Tay, and completed the journey south by rail.

The day at Sullom Voe had not been confined to snatching some much-needed sleep. We were also able to celebrate Sandy Glen's return to civilisation. He had left Sullom Voe as a smart naval officer on 3 May, but six weeks of rough living on Spitsbergen had brought a marked change of appearance. He had grown a straggly beard, his peaked hat had gone, and he was dressed in an Irvin flying suit that had seen better days. We could not supply a naval uniform, but he needed to be respectably dressed when reporting to the Admiralty. The best we could provide were facilities for a bath and a shave, then a clean RAF battledress and an RAF officer's forage cap. We soon relaxed now that tension was released, and all in the mess agreed that even the most senior officers in the Senior Service could not object to Sandy turning up in the uniform of the Junior Service. By now, the atmosphere was light-hearted and high-spirited, as a reaction to the gruelling events of the previous few days.

We were away from Sullom Voe for six days. Ronnie and I were able to take a brief spell of leave. But Tim and Sandy were occupied in a period of intense activity, with only a few home comforts available. The time of these two leaders at Sullom Voe had not been confined to celebration. They had revived their vision of a flight to the North Pole. The little matter of a world war could never deter men such as these.

CHAPTER EIGHT

Operation Gearbox

By the third week of June 1942, the planning staffs at three headquarters were still busy reappraising the situation in Spitsbergen. Sandy Glen's first duty on arrival in London was to report to the Director of Naval Intelligence. The information he brought with him must have been sufficiently welcome to offset his unorthodox attire. The resulting 'Report on Operation Fritham' was a model of clarity and precision. It outlined the specific factors that had contributed to the disaster. It gave details of the strengths and weaknesses of the survivors' situation, together with the possibility of realising the original objectives by sending reinforcements to Barentsberg. The assessment of the enemy strength in Spitsbergen was remarkably accurate (possibly confirmed by Enigma decrypts at Bletchley Park). It was known that a German W/T station and generator were in Hans Lund Hut and that the Germans were using as living accommodation the nearby Sysselmann House and the Post Office. The report also predicted the probable evacuation of German forces from Spitsbergen, their replacement by automatic weather-reporting equipment, and an extension of German aerial reconnaissance over the whole Arctic area.

Appraisal of this report quickly resulted in positive decisions at the Admiralty. It was soon realised that a further expediture of resources was justified to achieve the objectives of Fritham. Only a small landing force would be needed, but the risk of a second disaster had to be minimal. Operation Fritham was closed down and replaced by Operation Gearbox. Within Spitsbergen, activities on land would be under Norwegian command, but delivery of the reinforcements would be organised and implemented by the Royal Navy and co-ordinated with the movement of the PQ convoys to North Russia.

Sandy Glen and Tim Healy pointed out that, although the reconnaissance flights over the polar ice were not included in the listed objectives of Fritham, they were nevertheless an integral part of that operation. After Barentsberg had been reinforced, it would be possible to use Green Harbour as an advanced Catalina base. The equipment for this purpose had been prepared for the *Quest*, but the sailing from Akureyri in Iceland to Spitsbergen had been cancelled. It was not possible to include the personnel, stores and equipment in the Gearbox operation, but could they not be carried in a later PQ convoy? A faster-moving vessel could leave the slow convoy before reaching the Bear Island channel, deliver the supplies and rejoin the convoy in the Barents Sea.

The Admiralty did not have the jurisdiction to authorise the movement of RAF personnel and supplies, even though it could provide the means of transport. Thus Sandy and Tim took their proposals to the Headquarters of Coastal Command at Northwood. It is notable that the men concerned with the implementation were those who were making the running. Nevertheless, the RAF staff officers gave them the support they needed.

Thus, the prospect for the first RAF flight to the North Pole had been revived, with three somewhat different motives. The interest of the Admiralty was strictly strategic: a better understanding of the ice conditions over the sea route to North Russia. Sandy Glen had a wider view: the completion of a comprehensive survey of the movement of polar ice in the western hemisphere. Tim Healy's motive was simply to do it; he had been bitten by the exploration bug. But implementation of the flight would have to await events, primarily the successful outcome of Operation Gearbox and PQ17.

Meanwhile, there was more urgent work to be done. Information was required about the state of the ice to the south-west of Jan Mayen Island, partly because bad weather had prevented us from reviewing this during our flight of 15 June. The Admiralty also wanted to know how far north PQ17 could be routed after passing Jan Mayen. Sandy had to be taken back to Spitsbergen, to organise the reception of the reinforcements. These objectives could be obtained by flights from Sullom Voe to Spitsbergen via Iceland and Greenland.

This was the state of affairs when I joined Tim and Sandy at Northwood on 23 June, for a conference with Group Captain Dicken. I was not surprised to learn that Sandy had brought with him yet another of his Arctic colleagues. This was Major Andrew Croft, who had been with him in North East Land during 1935/36, and with Lindsay and Godfrey in Greenland during 1934. Croft was interested in seeing Scoresby Sound in Greenland from the air, as well as participating in the excitements of a jaunt to Spitsbergen. For our part, we were glad to have another Arctic expert on board, in case of emergencies.

Dicken outlined the latest developments. Operation Gearbox would be carried out by the cruiser *Manchester*, supported by the destroyer *Eclipse*, due to sail from Greenock the next day. The commander of the operation was Vice-Admiral S.S. Bonham-Carter of the 18th Cruiser Squadron, who had asked whether he could discuss matters with Glen and Healy before his departure. Dicken had provided a Lockheed Hudson to take us, after lunch, from Northolt to Abbotsinch. The station commander at this aerodrome had been asked to provide transport to Greenock, so that we could go aboard *Manchester* that evening, before returning to Abbotsinch for the night. The Hudson would then take us to Scatsta, an air strip near Sullom Voe. We would then be able to complete an ice reconnaissance to Greenland on 25 June and take Glen and Croft to Spitsbergen on 26/27 June. It was a tight programme, with no margins for contingencies or mishaps, but this did not surprise us. We were determined to carry it out.

It was a pleasant experience to be a passenger on a Hudson and to rely on someone else's navigation. The captain, Flight Lieutenant Sillives, did not let us down, and the Hudson crew delivered us safely. We stepped aboard *Manchester* with plenty of time for a long discussion, coupled with some naval hospitality. Our first concern was to carry out the correct procedure on going aboard, for we knew that we had to salute a mysterious entity called the 'Quarterdeck'. Tim's solution was to try to follow Sandy's lead, but in the confusion of arrival we lost sight of him. No one seemed to mind; perhaps their attention was focussed on more important matters.

Our hosts were preparing to embark on a thousand-mile journey, close to the ice edge, probably in continuous fog and without the benefit of sunsights, to make a landfall on a bleak coastline they had never seen before. Then they had to search for a narrow fjord in an area known to be patrolled by enemy aircraft. On arrival, they had to unload personnel and 116½ tons of equipment, probably without much assistance from those ashore. They had many questions to ask, of which only a few of the most important are related here.

Andrew Croft was fairly quiet, in the role of an interested observer. Sandy had become an unusually respectful lieutenant-commander on a serious naval occasion, and replied with very accurate factual information to the Vice-Admiral's questions about what he could expect to find at Barentsberg. Tim tried to be equally co-operative towards his naval colleagues, but his manner was more relaxed. I had the pleasure of hearing the navigating officer of the Senior Service express some doubts about the accuracy of his own navigation at the end of such a long voyage. So it was not only air navigators who experienced unease when approaching their landfalls! I can recall some of the questions:

'You have flown over the Arctic ice-pack. Can you tell us the limits of ice-free water to the north of Jan Mayen?'

Tim quoted the results of our reconnaissance on 14/15 June, and explained that we would have more up-to-date information on 27 June. We should be able to deliver a report to Seidisfjord in Iceland on 29 June, if the cruiser's departure from that port could be delayed until the next day.

'Have you any photographs of the Spitsbergen coastline to the north and south of Icefjord, to assist recognition on making a landfall?'

We had none with us, but Tim explained that we could take some on our next flight and he could bring the negatives with him. If the photographic section on the cruiser could develop and print them, he could explain what they depicted.

'Could the photographs be taken at low level, say at 100 feet, to show what the coastline might look like from the bridge?'

'Oh, yes,' Tim replied, turning to me and adding in a deliberately loud aside, 'We could climb up to that level if that's the height the Navy would prefer.' Tim was getting into his stride, and the atmosphere became noticeably less formal.

'Can you tell us about the pier facilities at Barentsberg, and the ice conditions there?'

Sandy replied to that one. He explained that the facilities were almost non-existent. There was only a pier, which was likely to be silted up, although it did have a crane. The pier would be ice-free, but the party might be hindered by ice floes floating down from the southern end of the fjord if the wind was southerly.

'Could you take some photographs of the pier, preferably vertical, to show whether there are any underwater obstructions which might impede unloading?'

Tim turned towards me, before replying, and his eyes were twinkling. 'Oh, yes,' he said. 'You could take some from the port blister while I do steep turns over the water's edge. If you wear that leather belt, Tommy could hold on to you. He'll make sure you don't fall out!'

Sandy explained that we would take Andrew Croft and himself to Spitsbergen on 26 June. When *Manchester* arrived five days later, he would contact them from the signal station half-way up the side of the fjord above Barentsberg and give them the latest information about enemy reconnaissance aircraft. There would be fewer than two dozen men at Barentsberg, so that little assistance could be expected from the survivors ashore. The Vice-Admiral assured him that the complete exercise would be handled by his own ship's company, with the help of the 54 Norwegian garrison troops under Lieutenant Gudim and 2nd Lieutenant Knudsen. He would also have available 46 assault troops under the command of Captain Dycker and three officers. The whole of the Norwegian force was under the command of Captain Ernest Ullring, DSO, of the Royal Norwegian Navy.

On our departure, Tim confirmed his promise to provide the Vice-Admiral with the position of the ice-edge, together with the photographs, at Seidisfjord on 29 June. Andrew's parting shot was to ask him for a lift back to Britain in the cruiser. It seems that he had only a short leave of absence from his unit!

It had been a short but highly successful example of inter-service co-operation, with respect and confidence displayed by all. We were back at Abbotsinch before midnight, ready for an early start the following day in the Hudson to Scatsta.

At Sullom Voe, it was all systems go. The Catalina needed an air test the same afternoon, in preparation for two long flights in the next three days. The first was expected to be full of interest; it would require close co-operation with the two ice observers, but otherwise should be fairly easy. The second would be more demanding and, towards the end, we could expect to be suffering from shortage of sleep.

The following day, 25 June, we slipped moorings at 13.10 hours and were airborne 11 minutes later. We then set course for Langanaes, the headland at the north-east corner of Iceland. The weather forecast was quite favourable, with an anti-cyclone to the west of Ireland moving slowly east while a depression over South Greenland moved north-east. An occlusion to the south-west of Iceland was expected to move north-east and reach Iceland later in the day. Winds were forecast as light and variable, with plenty of stratus cloud and stretches of fog towards Greenland.

We expected that the first leg of our journey would be uneventful, but at 13.45 hours a group of British trawlers opened fire on us. Fortunately for us, their markmanship was as poor as their aircraft recognition, but it gave Tim a chance to point out to Sandy that he was putting his life at risk every time he flew with us, particularly when itchy-fingered marine gunners were around. We dropped to 150 feet to exchange signals with the trawlers, but they did not co-operate and we climbed back to 720 feet and continued our journey.

We passed Cape Fuglo, on the north-east corner of the Faeroes, at 15.21 hours. From there to Iceland, the wind increased to nearly 20 knots and visibility decreased, with fog patches down to sea level. At 18.32 hours, we passed over Cape Langanaes and set course for Scoresby Sound, a huge fjord on the eastern coast of Greenland. Winds were lighter on the leeward side of Iceland and visibility deteriorated again. By 19.54 hours, at a height of 280 feet, there was thick sea fog beneath us. Beneath the fog were some stretches of drift ice, but the temperature remained above zero. Twenty minutes later, the ice had become pack ice, with waterlogged patches, and Sandy was moving to and from the blisters to mark the ice conditions on the navigation chart.

The radar picked up land 80 miles ahead, and we climbed above the sea fog to 750 feet. The coastline ahead was clear. We entered Scoresby Sound and everyone enjoyed the majestic splendour of the vistas that awaited us. The most appreciative member of our party was probably Andrew Croft, as he pointed out the mountains over which he had sledged eight years before. It was the sort of scenery that demanded photography, especially when a placid-looking iceberg floated out past Cape Brewster on its way to harass shipping in the Denmark Strait.

I stood at the open starboard blister for the next two hours, photographing the towering cliffs and the ice conditions along a 200 mile stretch of the coastline to the south of Cape Brewster. By 23.30 hours, it was time to return along an easterly track from Cape Nansen towards Iceland. We flew at the unusual height of 2,700 feet, to keep above the rising fog which partially obscured the drift ice below.

By 00.59 hours, we left the ice behind and Sandy's job was complete. The sea fog also disappeared, until Iceland drew near. Then it became so thick that we could only coast-crawl with the help

Cape Brewster, on Scoresby Sound in East Greenland, photographed from Catalina 'P for Peter' on 25 June 1942. The icebergs in the foreground are floating southwards towards the Denmark Strait.

A PB-Y Catalina of the US Navy landing at Reykjavik in Iceland. This photograph was taken in 1941.

of our radar. However, Tim and Ronnie knew the entrance to Eyja Fjord by this time, and we were safely moored at Akureyri by 02.35 hours on 26 June. It has been a fairly short flight for a long-range aircraft, just under 13½ hours, but it had been full of interest and not very tiring. This was important, since we were scheduled to take off again later in the day, to take Sandy and Andrew to Spitsbergen and carry out the photographic reconnaissance for *Manchester*, against the deadline of 29 June.

For a few hours, we enjoyed the hospitality of our Norwegian hosts in 330 Squadron, but Ronnie and I did not get much rest. It was our turn at 'anchor-watch' duty, and the sound of wavelets lapping against the duralumin hull was not conducive to sleep.

Security was still very tight. It must have been very annoying for the AOC-in-C Iceland to have a Catalina popping in and out of Akureyri without the captain divulging what he was doing, but Tim refused to say anything. Even the meteorological reports and forecasts we brought with us or which were transmitted to us in Iceland were arranged in Part 1, Part 2 and Part 3, instead of specifying the exact areas.

We were airborne in 'P for Peter' at 23.50 hours on the same day, and set course for Jan Mayen Island at a height of 270 feet. Conditions were excellent at first, with stratus cloud at about 3,000 feet and visibility of 35 miles. But an hour later we climbed to 900 feet to keep above a bank of dense sea fog, as forecast by our 'met' report. The nearer we flew to Jan Mayen the less we could see, but the faithful radar set picked up the high cliffs of the island at a distance of 60 miles and then guided us round the south-east headland to set course for Spitsbergen.

The sea fog continued all the way across the Greenland Sea. We spent the next few hours climbing and descending, taking drift readings when the surface of the sea was visible and hoping for some astro shots in the clearer air above. The log records that the distant-reading compass became unserviceable before 08.00 hours, probably with an electrical fault. However, the other magnetic compasses seemed reliable.

The radar picked up the coast of Spitsbergen at 08.10 hours. When the coast came in view, we dropped down to almost sea level to take some photographs for our friends on *Manchester*. The weather was still hazy and the tops of the mountains were chopped off by clouds, but the fog had cleared along the coastline, so that the photographs would be typical of what they could expect to see in a few days time.

When that job was done, 'P for Peter' was turned in an easterly direction to make a landfall at Bell Sound, a few miles to the south of Icefjord. Here we took photographs of Van Mijen Fjord. At the western end was Lowe Sound, a suitable anchorage for fleet tankers to refuel ships on PQ convoys. At the eastern end was Sveagruva, but we could see no sign of movement in the township. However, subsequent examination of the photographs showed tracks between some of the houses, indicating that some of the Norwegians were still in occupation.

Back we went to the entrance to Bell Sound, and for the next half hour photographs were taken of the coastline all the way round to Cape Linné, Green Harbour and Barentsberg. Recognition signals were exchanged with the ground party in their signal station near the mineshaft. Then we had 'fun' while I hung out of the port blister, taking the vertical photographs of the waters round the pier, for the benefit of Operation Gearbox. The leather belt proved an excellent safety strap, and it was reassuring to have the powerful Sergeant Thomas holding on to it.

The sheltered water of the fjord was ideal for a smooth landing, but we did not anchor. A boat came out to collect our two passengers, Glen and Croft, and it was not necessary to launch our dinghy. We were airborne again a few minutes later.

A month had passed since our last inspection of the German positions at Advent Bay. Sandy had told us about the overland reconnaissance, and it seemed desirable to find out whether there had been any further developments at the enemy airstrip, before operation 'Gearbox' got under way. We headed eastwards along Icefjord. Turning into Advent Bay, we could see that the flat stretch of ground between the sea and Longyearbyen was clear of snow, but that there were tracks on the ground leading towards the airstrip. We followed these, and they led us to an aircraft standing near a hut, with a truck and piles of stores alongside. Ronnie Martin was in a good position to relate the events:

It turned out to be a Ju88. Tim alerted the gunners to be ready to fire as soon as we were within range. I was carrying a private ciné camera and, of course, was sitting on the starboard side. The front gunner opened fire first, and then our starboard blister gunner. I

Ju88 at 'Bansö' airstrip on 27 June 1942, under machine gun fire from Catalina 'P for Peter'.

The same machine photographed in 1984.

could see clearly the tracer bullets entering the fuselage of the Ju88 from our blister gun. At the same time, I was using my ciné camera.

Tim continued flying and turned to starboard in front of the enemy aircraft. Then he turned right again and flew down the other side, and our gunners had another go. There did not seem to be any Germans around, although I understand that their records show that they fired back. We were quite a big target to hit, but suffered no damage at all.

Later in the war, I managed to have the cassettes of films taken on these flights processed by a chemist in Torquay. Some of them are a little over-exposed, but others are not too bad at all. For example, the tracers came out quite clearly on the film. Recently, I have had the film transferred into a video. Of course, it's black and white, but the advantage is that one can move it forward shot by shot, adjust the contrast and brilliance, and look carefully at the pictures.

Some 1,500 rounds were fired, mainly by the gunner in the starboard blister. It was satisfying for Tim to see that our previous practice sessions had proved effective, since firing sideways from a Catalina in flight required a large allowance for deflection, even at a stationary target. A photograph was taken from the RAF camera, showing smoke pouring out of the tail of the Ju88.

On our way back westwards, a message was dropped to the party at Barentsberg, telling them of our latest contribution to their welfare. But we could not linger any longer. Two hours of reconnaissance flying in the fjords of Spitsbergen had eaten into our precious reserves of fuel. There was still a long way to go for home – to whatever base would be designated as home. This called for some careful planning.

We expected to fly into sea fog during the first part of our journey southwards, so that there would be little chance of astro sights and the drift readings would be irregular and unreliable. Whether we had to return to Iceland or the Shetlands, there was likely to be poor visibility on arrival. The first radio report of the weather at Akureyri and Sullom Voe was due to be broadcast at Z + 18 hours, namely in seven hours time. 'Z' was a datum point, usually the time we had taken off. The most prudent action was to avoid Jan Mayen and to maintain a constant course southwards, so that seven hours later we would be equidistant from both bases.

For the next six hours, we repeated our practice on the outward leg, dropping through the sea fog to try to check the drift and then climbing up again in the vain hope of getting a sun sight.

At 18.32 hours, the expected message arrived: 'BASE UNFIT; AKUREYRI AND REYKJAVIK FIT.' We turned towards Iceland from a dead-reckoning position in which we had little confidence, with the sea fog stretching to the western horizon.

Needless to say, the sergeants in our crew were not unaware that their three officers were more interested than usual in making a landfall. The wireless operators were not surprised when the radar watch began long before our ETA, using the long-range beam aerials with an occasional switch to homing aerials, sometimes with an accompanying flat turn.

In the Catalina, the flight engineer could look down at the navigation table without moving from his panel of dials. David Baird noticed that, when no land was in sight, my dead-reckoning plot was approaching the coast of Iceland. He thought he should investigate. After checking the times on the plot, he asked with surprising cheerfulness:

'Are you lost?'

'The question should be "Are *we* lost?",' I replied.

'What are we going to do about it?' he queried.

'That depends on how much fuel we've got.'

'Plenty.'

'In that case, we can stay on this heading for another two hours, or until we make a landfall.'

'Where will that be?'

'Either Greenland or Iceland.'

'How shall we know which is which?'

'If it's green, it'll be Iceland. If it's icy it'll be Greenland.'

David made no further comment. He returned to his perch above me, looking quizzical. Shortly afterwards, the radar showed land 55 miles ahead. In due course, David showed his continued interest by calling down that he could see the land ahead.

'What colour?' I asked.

'Dark brown,' came his disgusted reply.

It was Cape Langanaes, in Iceland. We could not have hoped for a better landfall, but we were rather lucky. Later analysis of the log showed that there was a large landfall error. But we had made various allowances and assumptions, and I have always regarded that Arctic flight as a good one. It was an example of the difficulties of reconnaissance navigation at that time.

The northern coastline of Iceland was fog-bound but, with the help of our radar, we were able to coast-crawl to Eyja fjord, where we were moored up at 23.40 hours. The engines had been turning continuously for just over 24 hours.

By the time we had gone ashore, had a meal and sent off the necessary signals, it was 02.00 hours on 28 June. We were all very tired but Tim had to get his report to *Manchester* by the deadline of 29 June. The meteorological forecast confirmed our fear that we could not fly to Seidisfjord to meet the cruiser on that day. The prospect of a journey by road presented difficulties, but there was another possibility. At Akureyri, there was an armed trawler, the *Dorothy Gray*, which regularly patrolled the north coast of Iceland, undeterred by storms and fog. Arrangements were quickly made for Tim to complete his journey in this vessel, even though it was not the most comfortable method of travel for a land-lubber, particularly one who had had little sleep for two days. Tim declined our offers to accompany him. He thought we could best be of service by resting for two days, so that we would be fresh enough to fly back to Sullom Voe immediately after his return.

It must have appealed to Tim's sense of humour when he steamed into Seidisfjord in a weathered trawler, to heave-to alongside a large warship and to be welcomed aboard by a vice-admiral, regardless of his rather unkempt attire.

Only six days had passed since our discussion on board the cruiser at Greenock, but much had been packed into those few days. *Manchester* had left the Clyde at 21.00 hours on 25 June. Together with *Eclipse*, the cruiser had left Scapa at 09.00 hours on the 27 June, arriving in Seidisfjord at 18.35 hours the following day. Tim reached their anchorage at 16.45 hours on 29 June, only five hours before the two warships departed for Spitsbergen.

The up-to-the-minute report and the photographs that Tim took to the cruiser must have been extremely welcome. The Navy men now knew the conditions at Icefjord as well as those they could expect en route. Tim told them that the ice edge was running north-eastwards from Jan Mayen along a bearing of 042 degrees as far as 72 degrees latitude, where it turned northwards to form the ice-free area of Spitsbergen Bay. The sea fog that they were likely to experience should give them good cover from German reconnaissance aircraft, so that they should be able to refuel their accompanying destroyer in reasonable safety. They would also welcome the news that the German aircraft that normally appeared over Icefjord each day arrived between 02.00 hours and 05.00 hours, well before their own ETA.

Tim was soon back on the trawler, to endure the sea journey for a second time. Most people would have required a long rest after such a programme, which had been carried out with remarkable speed, but we were on our way back to Sullom Voe at 08.35 hours on 1 July. Tim had confidence in his crew and, in particular, he regarded Ronnie as a second captain rather than a second pilot. The other members of the crew were fully rested, and so he decided to return without delay. Besides, we were looking forward to a fortnight's leave in July, when he would have the opportunity to regain his strength at home.

We learned in due course that Operation Gearbox had been an outstanding success. Vice-Admiral Bonham-Carter delayed departure from Seidisfjord until 02.00 hours on 30 June so that, if sighted by U-boats in the vicinity of Jan Mayen, the Germans might think that his ships were covering convoy PQ17, which was en route to North Russia at the same time. When he reached the start of Spitsbergen Bay, he turned due north to maximise his distance from the Norwegian coastline and to get away from the convoy route. This enabled him to approach Icefjord from due west. Advantage was taken of thick fog on the evening of 1 July to refuel *Eclipse*. At 08.38 hours on the following morning Icefjord could be seen in conditions of excellent visibility. The two warships arrived off Barentsberg at 12.30 hours, to be greeted by a welcome message from the signal station:

ENEMY DAILY RECONNAISSANCE ABOUT 03.00 BUT NOT VISIT-
ING BARENTSBERG. ALSO SEEN OTHER TIMES AND ON 30 JUNE
AT 14.00. NO ENEMY LAND OR SEA ACTIVITY.

It proved impossible to moor alongside the pier because of silting, so that all personnel and equipment had to be taken ashore in boats. Both ships remained under way throughout the operation, with the ships' companies at anti-aircraft stations, but no enemy aircraft arrived to test their alertness. In just over six hours, 121 trips to the shore were made by 13 ships' boats, motor boats, a motor dinghy, a pinnace, cutters and whalers. Over 116 tons of equipment were manhandled by the ships' companies, aided by the 57 garrison troops who had been put ashore, without the port facilities normally needed for such work.

By 19.00 hours, the 50-man assault force was back on board, together with 13 extra passengers: Major Croft, Lieutenant Øi, Sub-Lieutenant Johannessen, three Mercantile Marine officers and seven ratings. The two ships were then ready to leave Green Harbour. It had been a daring exploit, but by brilliant planning, organisation and performance, the operation had been completed successfully. Barentsberg had been reinforced without the enemy being any the wiser.

When Captain Ullring stepped ashore at Barentsberg on 2 July to command the Norwegian force, his primary aim was not economic, as had been that of his predecessor, Lieutenant Colonel Sverdrup. The purpose was strategic, to re-establish Norwegian sovereignty over the archipelago. The new Military Govenor already had a reputation for courage, discipline and determination. In 1941, he had assumed control of all meteorological stations on Jan Mayen Island and Greenland. As captain of the patrol ship *Fridhjof Nansen* he had shown determination and tact in handling Arctic encounters with Danish, Norwegian and German meteorological units.

However, Barentsberg needed the attentions of someone who was more than a distinguished naval officer, and Ullring soon exhibited extra qualities. The area was a mining settlement and had all the visible trappings of that industry. It had been evacuated hurriedly and subsequently had been subjected to aerial bombing. There were frozen corpses of horses, cattle, pigs and dogs, lying where they had been slaughtered. Overhead, there was the smoke from still-smouldering coal dumps. The place was dismal, deserted and desolate. Yet Ullring found some more appealing aspects to describe in his first despatch from Spitsbergen, as he looked across the fjord at the beautiful snow-clad hills and mountains in the evening Arctic sunshine.

The first job after *Manchester* and *Eclipse* had departed was to obliterate all indications that a new force had arrived. Cranes and platforms were removed from the quayside, boats moored and hidden, and stores distributed and camouflaged. Next, attention was turned to anti-aircraft defences, but that brought a major disappointment. No ammunition belts could be found for the Colts, and without these the guns were useless. Priority was thus given to the much heavier Oerlikon guns, first setting them up in improvised sites and then finding more permanent stations. By 5 July, four Oerlikons and four Brownings had been mounted, with gun crews

(*Left*) Captain Ernst Ullring, DSO, of the Royal Norwegian Navy, photographed in 1944.

Dr Etienne (*seated, wearing hat*) talking to Leutnant Schütze at 'Bansö' airstrip before the German evacuation in July 1942.

drilled and ready for action.

While this activity was progressing, the enemy left them unmolested, although there was plenty of aerial activity. At 01.00 hours on 3 July, an enemy aircraft was heard flying along Icefjord, returning an hour later after presumably landing at Longyearbyen. But the airmen paid no attention to Green Harbour. Towards mid-day, a Ju52 transport followed the same path. Clearly, some changes were taking place over to the east.

Indeed, the Germans at Bansö were concentrating their attention on the evacuation. They had reported to Banak the attack which we in 'P for Peter' had made on 27 June; the Ju88 had been so badly peppered by machine gun bullets that it could not be repaired. It was, of course, the machine that had suffered two damaged propellers after Leutnant Wagner had landed it on 14 June. The Germans stated that they had hit the Catalina with return fire, but we suffered no damage.

On 30 June, however, there was better news for Banak. The airstrip had dried out sufficiently for use by light aircraft and by Ju52s. This brought an immediate intensification of activity. Further supplies were flown in, so that another winter station could be set up later in the autumn and the remaining personnel could be evacuated. These events were witnessed by a small group of Norwegians sent by Lieutenant Lund to try to destroy the German W/T station at Advent Bay. The men did not achieve their objective but the captain of *Eclipse* was told of the enemy activity.

When the peaks in southern Spitsbergen were clear of cloud, the pilots of the German aircraft preferred the more direct path over the mountains. When visibility was poor and the aircraft were heavily laden, the pilots kept to the lower coastal route, which passed Barentsberg. The fog and low cloud which had greeted the *Isbjørn* and *Selis* turned out to be to their detriment. The good visibility which welcomed *Manchester* and *Eclipse* benefited their security, for the German aircraft stayed away from the western end of Iceford. The fortunes of war favoured the British warships.

By 9 July, the German evacuation was complete. The last aircraft to leave, piloted by Rudolf Schütze, carried back to Banak the meteorologist who had master-minded the provision of weather information from Advent Bay since autumn 1941, Dr Etienne. He had good cause to be satisfied with his work. Dr Moll's four-man team had provided a constant flow of reports during the months of winter darkness. Now arrangements had been made to continue the service even after their departure. They had left behind a fully-operational weather machine, the faithful Kröte, carefully installed on a well-chosen site at Hjorthamn on the northern side of Advent Bay.

Thus, by this time both the Allies and the Germans had attained their immediate aims in Icefjord. Neither, however, was precisely aware of the objectives and achievements of the other. The next fortnight would show how the advantage had swung.

CHAPTER NINE

Consolidation

Within a week of the arrival of the reinforcements at Barentsberg, a firm foundation was secured. A disciplined routine was established, a meteorological station was set up, and an effective wireless communication established with Britain. The latter proved one of the most beneficial assets, for the men did not have to suffer the strain of isolation. Captain Ullring exchanged detailed information with his home base. He requisitioned ammunition clips for the Colts, made arrangements for a Catalina delivery run, reported signs of enemy activity, and arranged recognition signals.

The men of Operation Fritham had made a valiant response to their misfortune, but much of their energy had been spent on survival and making do with minimal resources. They could keep up their morale only by believing that help would come eventually. The experience and local knowledge of these men were invaluable to the new arrivals, who admired the fortitude and tenacity of their predecessors. Nevertheless, Captain Ullring reported that a few of the earlier men seemed too afraid of aircraft; he referred to this as 'bomb shock', presumably linking it with the 'shell shock' of exhausted troops in World War One.

The two British liaison officers were in the privileged position of being directly involved with both Norwegian commanders, while remaining of independent status. They witnessed both operations and could now see the second expedition moving steadily towards the objectives of the first. It was evident to them that Ullring was indeed a most effective commander. This view was also shared by the Norwegian medical officer, who included these remarks in a report dated 15 September 1942:

> I cannot let this opportunity go without mentioning the gratitude which I feel towards Commander Ullring, DSO, for his inspiring fighting spirit which he transferred to the men and officers. I cannot but note the valuable effect his leadership has had on the mental state and courage which all of us have benefited from. If

but the same spirit will last I have no fear for the winter coming.

While Sandy Glen shared in this high opinion of the new commander he was also, by 15 July, looking forward to our arrival in 'P for Peter', so that more detailed preparations could be made for the polar flights. But these required co-operation from London, such as the provision in Spitsbergen of fuel, moorings, chassis, stores and the like. Unknown to him, other events in the Arctic during the first fortnight in July made the provision of such equipment extremely unlikely. Attention had to be concentrated on the grim results of the next PQ convoy.

When Vice-Admiral Bonham-Carter left Barentsberg on 2 July, three options were open to him. He could return to Seidisfjord in Iceland; he could try to contact the four heavy cruisers which formed the Support Force for convoy PQ17; or he could join the heavy ships of the Covering Force. He chose the last, and joined the Home Fleet on the evening of 3 July, far to the west of Bear Island.

Convoy PQ17 had left Iceland on 27 June, consisting of 35 merchant ships, six destroyers, four corvettes, three mine-sweepers, four anti-submarine trawlers, two submarines, two converted AA ships and three rescue ships. The convoy and its close escorts passed Jan Mayen Island on 1 July. During the three weeks since our ice report of 14 June, the ice edge had receded further northwards, so that the convoy could sail well to the north of Bear Island. It was when the convoy was in this most vulnerable position that the Admiralty had grounds to believe that a major threat was imminent.

Grossadmiral Raeder put into effect a surprise move, named 'Rösselsprung' or 'Knight's Move'. He sent the battleship *Tirpitz* northwards to Alten fjord in Norway, together with the cruisers *Hipper* and *Lützow* and the pocket battleship *Admiral Scheer*, during the first days of July. To counter such a menace, there was a Support Force consisting of four Allied cruisers hovering to the north of the convoy, but the Covering Force of battleships and a carrier was to the west of Bear Island. The Admiralty was reluctant to send the Covering Force to the east of Bear Island, where the warships would have been exposed without air cover to torpedo bombers and U-boats. The Support Force was not capable of combating the *Tirpitz*, which might in any event have been able to slip past the Allied ships and create havoc in the shipping lanes of the Atlantic. *Tirpitz* had not in fact sailed, but on 4 July, with conflicting intelligence on which to base their decision, the Admiralty ordered the convoy to scatter when it had just passed Hope Island.

The Luftwaffe and the U-boats could then pick off the merchant ships, almost at will. Only eleven vessels reached Archangel, and the flotsam of war was spread across the inhospitable waters of the Barents Sea. When the escorts obeyed instructions and turned west, the merchant seamen thought that they were running away and their anger knew no bounds. One of the results was a large number of ship-wrecked mariners needing rescue in the Barents Sea. The response to that need was one of the many functions of Coastal Command reconnaissance aircraft. Several Catalinas had been sent round to North Russia in connection with the passage of PQ17, and it is interesting to follow the fortunes of one of these.

On 12 July, 210 Squadron at Sullom Voe received orders to send out a Catalina for two objectives. Firstly, the crew had to deliver supplies, including Colt ammunition clips, to the Gearbox force at Spitsbergen. Then they had to fly 100 miles east of South Cape to Hope Island and from there along the edge of the icepack to the prudent limit of endurance. The final part of the first objective was to land in North Russia, either at Grasnaya on the Kola Inlet or Lake Lakhta near Archangel. After resting, the crew had to carry out the second objective. This involved flying to the point where they had left their previous ice reconnaissance and continuing it to a point midway between Novaya Zemlya and Franz Josef Land, at which point they would have reached 78 degrees North. Then they had to return to North Russia via Cape Nassau on the west coast of Novaya Zemlya. Such a flight over the Barents Sea included a hunt for survivors of PQ17 and their possible rescue.

At the time, Tim Healy and his crew were on leave, while their Catalina "P for Peter' was undergoing a maintenance check at Gourock. The flights were thus carried out by Catalina 'N', with Flight Lieutenant G.G. Potier as captain and Flight Sergeant J.S. Liddle as navigator. The first sortie started from Sullom Voe at 13.59 hours on 13 July. An enemy aircraft was sighted at 20.05 hours, but this abandoned pursuit 25 minutes later. The Catalina arrived over Barentsberg at 00.25 hours the following day, to be greeted with machine gun fire which holed the tail and one wing. Apparently two gun crews misunderstood Captain Ullring's instructions not to fire. The Catalina then exchanged recognition signals and landed in Green Harbour, to off-load packages and messages. The schedule was so tight that the crew had to take off within ten minutes, there being no time for them to express an opinion about the shooting.

The Catalina reached Hope Island at 03.10 hours but the crew could keep track of the ice edge only by flying at 200 feet, below the cloud base. There were several leads running northwards but it was inadvisable to follow any of them and risk heavy icing. At the limit of endurance, they turned southwards to make for Archangel, and after a while sighted five lifeboats with about 40 men on board. The sea swell was too heavy for a landing, but the crew dropped food and cigarettes wrapped in camera covers inside a Mae West life-jacket. This was seen to be picked up, and the Catalina crew flashed a message of encouragement before heading to the White Sea. They reached Lakhta at 13.40 hours on 14 July and lost no time in making a report to the Senior British Naval Officer (SBNO).

It had been a 24-hour flight, but the crew were off again at 16.25 hours on the next day. Their duties were to complete the ice reconnaissance and look for more survivors of PQ17. Their final report shows the painstaking and comprehensive details with which they completed the first task, giving the Admiralty the precise information required for planning the next stage of the convoy movements.

On the return journey, the crew flew along the southern shoreline of Novaya Zemlya. At 07.30 hours they sighted a ship at anchor in the centre of Moller Bay. The Catalina landed and taxied up to it. It proved to be a Cam ship *Empire Tide*, which had collected 42 survivors from other ships and was expecting more shortly afterwards. The Catalina took off again and almost immediately sighted and communicated with a ship aground at the southern end of Moller Bay, the *Winston Salem*.

The Catalina was back at Lake Lakhta at 13.55 hours on 16 July to make a report, which confirmed that the sea was ice-free from Moller Bay to Cape Kanin at the entrance to the White Sea. A small force of corvettes left Archangel on the same day and successfully rescued all the survivors, as well as many others.

The Catalina was airborne yet again the following day, on the return journey to Sullom Voe. In the period of five days, Flight Lieutenant Potier and his crew had been in the air for 63 hours and completed all their objectives. Even by the standards of the flying boats of Coastal Command, it was a remarkable performance.

The Colt ammunition clips were exactly what Captain Ullring needed to complete his preparations for an assault on the German positions at Advent Bay. He set off at 12.15 hours on 15 July in a motor-cutter with a Colt mounted on board. He carried ten men, including Sergeant Knutsen and Rating Branther, who knew Advent Bay well. Later, Lieutenant Lund with another small party set off in a whaler fitted with an outboard motor. In the early evening, a search of Advent Bay confirmed their earlier belief that the enemy had flown. There were several indications that they intended to return; the W/T and other instruments were in good working order, there were plenty of stores, the accommodation was ready for reoccupation, and no attempt had been made to demolish the Ju88 which we had peppered on 1 July.

One of the requirements of an automatic meteorological unit was that it had to be sited in an exposed position to report local data. The Kröte that the Germans had installed at Advent Bay was placed close to the shore near Hjorthamn, and the Norwegians discovered it almost immediately. It was dismantled and taken back to Barentsberg for onward transfer to Britain as soon as transport could be arranged.

Lieutenant Lund was left behind to guard Longyearbyen with a small detachment, armed with two Colts and two Brownings mounted in suitable positions. They did not have to wait long before going into action. The signals transmitted by the Kröte were picked up at Banak for the first week after its installation, but then it suddenly went off the air. A Ju88 was sent over Advent Bay to try to find out what was wrong. It flew over the site at 04.00 hours on 20 July, to find that the station had been destroyed. Moreover, when Lund's gunners opened fire the Germans knew that some sort of enemy commando unit must have taken over. The Norwegians heard the aircraft returning over Sveagruva and thus they knew the Germans at Banak must have been alerted.

The men in Barentsberg were not surprised when another Ju88 turned southwards into Green Harbour on the following day. It was met by heavy fire from the Oerlikons and left the fjord with smoke pouring from its port engine and a large hole in one wing-tip. Nevertheless, the pilot managed to return to Banak, where he reported the changed situation. The German fears of a seaborne reinforcement had proved to be justified, although the nature and strength of the opposition was not known precisely.

The visits by the Ju88s prompted Lieutenant Lund to take some precautions against a return in strength. Some of the papers which the Norwegians had discovered in the huts at Longyearbyen indicated that the Germans considered the ground too soft for safe landings during the summer months. Nevertheless, it was desirable to make the airstrip even less attractive. All landing markers were removed, obstacles were scattered along its length, and a few trenches dug. Lund then felt secure against an attack from airborne soldiers.

Further searches, made in huts along Adventdalen, revealed another radio transmitter/receiver in good working order, as well as further supplies of stores. The Norwegians were able to build up a clear picture of how the weather station and the airstrip functioned.

While Lieutenant Lund consolidated his position at Advent Bay, Captain Ullring set out in the other direction. He sailed in the motor cutter to Bell Sound, Van Mijenfjord and Braganza Bay, to visit the other Fritham survivors at Sveagruva. His presence and the weapons that he brought with him gave an important fillip to the morale of these men. Ullring brought nine of these men back to Barentsberg, to strengthen his forces for the next expedition.

At Banak in Norway, the Germans realised that their plans for automatic weather data from Advent Bay during the summer and a manned station during winter had been badly upset. Major Vollrath Wibel had recently arrived in Banak, entrusted with new duties in the Icefjord region of Spitsbergen. He and Dr Erich Etienne needed more precise information about the nature and extent of the disruption. It was arranged that a Ju88 should take them on a reconnaissance flight over Advent Bay on 23 July. This was flown by one of the most experienced Arctic airmen, Leutnant Heinz Wagner, accompanied by a wireless operator, Unteroffizier Heinrich Voss.

In contrast to the strict radio silence maintained by the reconnaissance aircraft of Coastal Command, the aircraft of Wettererkundungsstaffel 5 made full use of the radio when flying in the Arctic and kept in regular contact with Banak. On this occasion, the radio communications continued until the Ju88 reached the entrance to Icefjord. Then there was silence.

The Ju88 flew at very low level across Advent Bay towards the site of the Kröte near the shore at Hjorthamn. Waiting patiently was Nils Langbak, a gunner from the sunken *Selis*, with his Colt cocked ready for action. He fired only ten rounds. The German aircraft seemed to be doing a steep turn, close to the ground, while those on board searched for clues about their silent weather station. Within seconds, the Ju88 had crashed and exploded, killing all on board, close to the site that they had been inspecting. Examination of the wreckage revealed that the lower part of one engine had been pierced by two rounds. At that part of Advent Valley, the slopes of Hiorthfjellet were crossed by funicular cables, and it is possible that the aircraft might have collided with one of these after being hit. Be that as it may, the gunner from the *Selis* had avenged the sinking of his ship two months before.

The identities of the four occupants of the Ju88 were established from correspondence in their pockets. They were buried in separate graves, close to the scene of the crash, and crosses set up.*

The loss of the aircraft came as a severe shock to the German squadron. The men at Banak had not only lost experienced leaders, but they did not know where or how. Low-level searches of the area brought no clues, except to confirm that their enemy had gained control and that the airstrip at Bansö could no longer be used. The German airmen knew that they would be unable to return to Spitsbergen without a major allocation of resources, and that would not be possible in 1942. They had lost control in Spitsbergen.

A new era had begun for the Norwegians. They had consolidated their position and suffered no losses. Morale was high. Valuable information had been found, including signals references and code books. The automatic weather recoding equipment had been brought back to Barentsberg, as well as instruments from the Ju88. They even found some aviation fuel at Bansö. The latter caused Sandy Glen to wonder if the enemy had unexpectedly solved the problem of providing the Catalina with fuel for the polar flight; it would have to be checked for quality.

A steady flow of information was fed back to London by Major Whatman's team of wireless operators. In London, the Admiralty was busy making comprehensive plans for the next PQ convoy to North Russia, due to sail from Loch Ewe at the beginning of September. The Navy hoped to use one of the Spitsbergen fjords, Lowe Sound, for refuelling some of the convoy's escorts. There were obviously benefits to be gained by sending further reinforcements to Barentsberg. Again, the movement would have to be handled by British cruisers, their movements being co-ordinated with the planning of the convoy. Lieutenant-Commander Glen was needed back in London for further consultations. It was time for a Catalina flight to Barentsberg to be arranged.

The first fortnight in July was quiet for the crew of 'P for Peter'. We

---

*The historian Franz Selinger has recorded that the bodies were later exhumed and reburied in the graveyard of Botn-Rognan near Bodö.

took the aircraft to Gourock on 5 July and went on leave while it was being overhauled. During the flight for Operation Gearbox, decorations had been gazetted. Tim Healy received a DSO, the highest award that could be granted for this type of work. Sergeant George Victor Kingett, the first wireless operator, received a DFM. Unexpectedly, I received a DFC.

On return to Gourock on 18 July, we found that a new 'toy' had been fitted to the aircraft. This was a navigational aid, called an Air Position Indicator, which had recently been invented. A prototype was fitted in 'P for Peter', and we were required to report on its effectiveness for Coastal Command operations.

The purpose of the instrument was to overcome plotting errors, since the courses drawn on a navigator's chart might not take sufficient account of movements of the aircraft during flight. Errors could arise because of unsteady courses flown by the pilot, manoeuvring and turning, and changes of airspeeds while climbing and descending. These difficulties were more likely to occur in aircraft where pilots had to take rapid avoiding action, rather than in flying boats. On the other hand, our type of flying could provide an excellent testing ground for a prototype.

The gearing mechanism was packed into a neat little box, placed near the navigator on his table. One did not need to understand the mechanism to operate the device. All the navigator had to do in flight was to set on its dials the latitude and longitude of the departure point, and then to make adjustments for changes in magnetic variation as the aircraft flew its course. No matter in what direction the aircraft turned and at what speeds it flew, the dials on the instrument would tick over, showing the latitude and longitude of the aircraft on the assumption that it had not been affected by wind velocity. When the navigator discovered his ground position, either visually or by calculation, he could then work out the wind velocity that had affected the aircraft.

Since all instruments, particularly prototypes, are liable to error or breakdown, the navigator was urged to keep his own manual air plot in the usual way, and to compare the two results, before deciding which to use before adding a wind vector to calculate a dead-reckoning position.

We realised at the outset that there would be difficulties with the instrument on our long northerly flights. A journey from Sullom Voe to Icefjord covered eighteen degrees of latitude, moving from one chart to another on several occasions. It was extremely tedious to transfer air positions and then refer back to changing latitude scales in order to plot the wind vector. In fact, we plotted tracks, not courses, on such flights.

Our first job was to test this instrument in flight. We did this by flying on very steady courses from the Shetlands to the Faeroes and introducing various manoeuvres on the way back. Our normal methods showed that our dead-reckoning positions were very close to the final landfalls, whereas the new instrument gave us dead-reckoning positions with about a mile extra error.

The first opportunity to test the new instrument on an Arctic flight came on 26 July but we were recalled to base after only an hour. The weather had closed in, and it was not until 09.00 hours on 29 July that we were able to take off again. One urgent reason for the flight was to take some anti-tetanus serum and other supplies to the Gearbox party at Barentsberg. The other important purpose was to bring back Sandy Glen for consultations about the next operation, which had the code 'Gearbox 2'. In addition, there were several items of equipment and information that were ready for collection.

The flight followed the pattern of previous ones, with plenty of fog, although on this occasion there was less high cloud and we were able to make more use of astro sights. The Air Position Indicator was used but, with the extra work entailed, it was more of a chore than an assistance to us.*

Sandy was ready to come aboard with all his equipment and as keen as us for an early departure. We were back at Sullom Voe before mid-day on 30 July and would normally have been asleep soon afterwards. On this occasion, however, Tim and Sandy had too much to discuss. Both were still keen to attempt a polar flight and the climatic conditions were such that it could not be delayed beyond August. Sandy was confident that the Norwegians were sufficiently well established in Icefjord for Green Harbour to be used as an advanced seaplane base. There was no longer any need for two flights, and the objectives could be achieved in a single successful attempt.

Less fuel would be needed for only one flight, while economies might be possible in equipment and ground personnel. It was doubtful, however, whether supplies could be shipped to Spits-

---

*Nevertheless, the Air Position Indicator (API) became part of the standard equipment on heavy aircraft of Bomber Command later in the war.

bergen in time. For military and strategic purposes, it was difficult to justify even one flight across the 80th parallel. Nevertheless, Tim was not to be deterred by such considerations and his enthusiasm was infectious. Wing Commander H.B. 'Johnnie' Johnson, who had taken over command of 210 Squadron, seemed to be equally keen on the project. But there would have to be representations to the Admiralty and to Coastal Command HQ.

It was arranged that we should fly 'P for Peter' to Calshot, near Southampton, with all the equipment that Sandy had to deliver to the Admiralty Intelligence Division. We were granted special permission to fly down the east coast as far as the Wash and then cut across country to the south coast. It must have been the first time that some members of the Home Guard and the Royal Observer Corps had ever seen a Catalina. The seagulls at Calshot also found our aircraft something of a novelty, for they soon formed a long line along the leading edge of our mainplane. We were there for the next eighteen days and, judging from the evidence that they left behind, the gulls must have spent most of their time on their new perch. In the crew, we had the pleasure of more leave. Tim and Sandy had homes in London and were able to mix their leaves with more serious business as they sought support for their modified polar ambitions.

At the Admiralty, plans for the next convoy to North Russia, PQ18, were well advanced. These had to be more comprehensive than those made for its unfortunate predecessor, PQ17. In addition, preparations were being made to send further supplies and reinforcements of personnel to Barentsberg. These were to include 40 Husky dogs, three 40 mm Bofors guns, two tractors, boats, wireless and direction-finding equipment, and other stores for the winter. All this weighed over 200 tons. Vice-Admiral Bonham-Carter would again be in command. Operation Gearbox 2 would be carried out by two cruisers, *Cumberland* and *Sheffield*, with the destroyer *Eclipse* again in attendance. Once again, Sandy Glen was appointed the British liaison officer ashore. He realised immediately that the stores did not include those necessary for an advanced Catalina base. But Tim was not too dismayed at this news, for he was developing some other ideas for which only Coastal Command sanction would be required.

Tim's views were quite simple. If we could not carry out the original plan to fly to the North Pole from Spitsbergen, why not try a round trip from Akureyri in Iceland? It was a lot further, a 3,000 mile journey, but Tim had been keeping a record of our fuel consumption on the long Arctic flights. He estimated that, given favourable conditions, we could keep airborne for over 31 hours. In perfect conditions, we could reach the North Pole and return. In less perfect conditions, we should get fairly close. In poor conditions, we would have to turn round and abandon the attempt. Tim's eyes were gleaming at the prospect.

At Coastal Command HQ at Northwood, Tim and Sandy were delighted to find that there was still a spirit of adventure in the corridors of power. The flight was approved, provided certain priorities were satisfied first. The Admiralty had to be assured that Sandy Glen would be back in Barentsberg in time to prepare for the arrival of the cruisers and the destroyer early in September. Also 'P for Peter' had to be back at Sullom Voe early in September for a very important operation. This was the detachment of ten Catalinas of our squadron to North Russia, as part of the RAF force detailed to support convoy PQ18. If these requirements were met, the staff officers gave Tim their full backing. The official justification for the flight was the ice reconnaissance that would be carried out along the Greenland coastline, coupled with navigational research and experience into high latitude and polar flying. But there can be little doubt that the staff officers were also spurred on by fellow-feeling with Tim's enthusiasm.

The attempt on the North Pole was to be regarded as a flight to the 'prudent limit of endurance'. The staff officers did not expect the Catalina to go further than 86 to 88 degrees North. They emphasised that Tim, as captain of the aircraft, was in sole command, and that he was being *permitted* to undertake the flight rather than ordered to do so. It was his decision about fuel consumption that would be paramount. The staff officers also suggested that, after the Catalina had returned to Iceland, Sandy should be taken to Spitsbergen via North-East Greenland, to examine the normal outflow path of the polar ice.

After the run to Spitsbergen, the Catalina should return to Sullom Voe and take part in the Russian detachment. Then one more duty would be required, to bring Sandy home for the winter or whatever other duties awaited him; this could probably be done on our return flight from North Russia.

It was a tight programme, but we had become accustomed to such pressure as part of the normal pattern of Arctic flying. Although Tim did not guarantee to take Sandy to the North Pole, the explorer knew that if anyone could do it, that man was Flight Lieutenant Dennis

Edward Healy, DSO. Meanwhile, the crew of 'P for Peter' knew that their captain had completed over 900 hours of operational flying and that the programme ahead would bring him to the end of his tour of 1,000 hours. It would be a fitting climax to six months of intensive effort.

CHAPTER TEN

The North Pole

We returned in 'P for Peter' to Sullom Voe on 18 August, knowing that there were only a couple of days in which to complete preparations for the long-delayed flight to the North Pole. However, our blithe hopes that the final arrangements would not be interrupted by other operational duties were dashed immediately. The required sortie was only a short flight of seven and a half hours, but it demonstrated the wide range of duties that flying boat squadrons could be called upon to perform.

Danish trawlers were continuing to fish in the North Sea, in spite of the air-sea attacks by Coastal Command's strike aircraft against German convoys in these waters. It was suspected that some of these vessels were carrying Germans in order to transmit warning radio messages about the movements of our strike aircraft towards the enemy coasts. Investigation and, if necessary, punitive action was advocated. Unfortunately, there were too few warships available for this purpose. Someone had the bright idea of calling on the resources of the flying boat squadrons.

Two Catalinas of 210 Squadron were ordered to fly to the Dogger Bank in the middle of the North Sea, where the Danish fishing boats were operating. A boarding party consisting of our station commander, who was a group captain, and members of his marine craft section, were to fly with the senior captain. If this captain considered that the sea conditions were safe, he was to land alongside one of the fishing boats and supervise the transfer of the boarding party. The other Catalina was to remain aloft and give whatever supporting action was considered necessary. Tim was the obvious choice for the senior captain. Perhaps someone had heard that we carried a collapsible dinghy.

There was much raucous laughter in the officers' mess about the proposed operation, during the evening. But in the Operations Room the following morning, our squadron commander managed to keep his face sufficiently straight to tell us that the operation had to be taken seriously. However, he instructed Tim that on no account was he to risk losing the valuable 'P for Peter'. The warning was not really necessary, for Tim was far too keen on the polar flight to risk everything on such an impossible exercise.

Both Catalinas slipped moorings at 13.05 hours on 20 August. We were airborne in 'P for Peter' at 13.15 hours. The other aircraft, 'F for Freddie', took off three minutes later. We had hoped to fly together but the inevitable happened and we lost sight of each other in the swirling mist. A further suggestion that we should transmit a homing signal when we reached the ships had been indignantly rejected by the crew of 'F for Freddie', as a slur on their ability. Thus a race began to be the first to find the trawlers.

As we drew near the Dogger Bank, the fog thickened and the sea swell worsened. The radar picked up the first trawler on the far side of the Bank and then a second one three miles to the south-east. Both were flying the Danish flag and neither replied to our Aldis signals, although they altered course to the direction we required. The bows of both were plunging into the heavy swell, with foaming white water pouring over the decks.

During the outward flight, one member of our crew had offered odds of ten to one against our being able to effect a landing. These odds were increased to a hundred to one over the target, when he had seen the group captain's face after inspecting the surface of the sea through the bomb aimer's window in the bows. Tim decided that a landing was totally impracticable and the station commander readily concurred. Moreover, even if we had succeeded in landing, no one could see how the boarding party could transfer to the trawler, even with the whole-hearted co-operation of the ship's crew. Our dinghy was capable of carrying two men who could, with some difficulty, paddle ashore in sheltered waters. The scheme was derisory.

At 17.22 hours we signalled 'TRAWLERS MET' and 27 minutes later notified Sullom Voe that we were returning home. Both signals were intercepted by the other Catalina, which then had the mortification of turning back without having seen any trawlers. There was no shortage of ribaldry in the mess that evening. Fortunately we had brought back photographs to substantiate our sighting.

For security reasons we never talked about a flight to the North Pole, and very few members of our squadron were aware of this project. On the rare occasions when it had to be mentioned in public, it was referred to as 'the northern flight'.That is how it was entered in our flying log books.

The Arctic flights we had carried out since May had all been far enough from the Pole to permit the use of magnetic compasses, although some of these had been especially adapted to cope with the lower horizontal strength of the earth's magnetic field. This had confirmed our belief that high latitude air navigation (between 60 and 80 degrees North) could be carried out on the same principles as in more southerly latitudes. It merely required greater care, particularly in using the changing distance scales on the Mercator charts. We had used standard dead-reckoning techniques, supported by aids such as astro sights, airborne radar and, occasionally, radio bearings by using the direction-finding loop aerial.

At 10.45 hours on 21 August 1942, moorings were slipped in the same way as on all other flights and, a few minutes later, 'P for Peter' was on its way to Iceland. At last, we were to have an opportunity to fly to the North Pole.

Sandy Glen had come with us to the Operations Room, but there had been little discussion. It was still being treated as a secret mission, so that all we needed was a weather report. We knew that the odds were loaded against a successful completion of the enterprise. If the weather did not permit departure from Akureyri to the North Pole the following day, or if it turned against us on the way northwards – for the forecast could be little better than guesswork – the project would have to be abandoned. There would be no opportunity for a second attempt.

The main object of the flight could no longer be regarded of much benefit to the Admiralty or the convoy route to Russia. We considered that the flight had four objectives:

1. The completion of our researches into the techniques of air navigation.

2. A reconnaissance of the polar ice between Greenland and the North Pole.

3. An examination of the effect of the Transpolar Drift and the East Greenland current on the movement of ice along the east coast of Greenland.

4. The collection of meteorological data, the photographing of the east coast of Greenland, and an examination into the behaviour of magnetic compasses.

The sergeants in our crew were aware that they were about to share in a trip into the unknown, but they had unshaken confidence in their officers 'up front'. All previous targets had been reached. We had always returned safely to base, and there seemed no reason to think otherwise on this occasion. Sandy seemed supremely confident; he even managed to keep his normal exuberance in check. Tim was quietly thoughtful and responsible, while Ronnie and I played our sincere parts as his loyal supporters.

'P for Peter' was waterborne safely at Akureyri and we turned in early in preparation for the polar flight on the next day. We were out of our beds before dawn to find everything shrouded in fog. The weather forecast for the northern part of the journey, specially sent from London to cover 36 hours, was favourable. However, we still needed assurance from the local meteorological officer that the northern coast of Iceland would be clear of fog on our return from the Pole 30 hours later. Security considerations prevented us from telling him why this information was so important to us. Unfortunately, at this stage he could not be other than pessimistic, and Tim had no option but to defer take-off.

This delay was troublesome from the point of view of navigation, for it was desirable to time the flight so that it was correctly geared to the movement of the sun around the horizon. It would take fifteen hours to reach the Pole and fifteen hours to come back. Ideally, the sun should be directly behind us or directly in front of us as we approached the Pole. Thus an astro position line obtained from it, at right angles to its direction, would give a latitude check. At intermediate positions, the sun would be in either the western or eastern skies six hours before or after reaching the Pole. This would thus give us a longitude check on the east coast of Greenland.

Akureyri and the east coast of Greenland lie between 15 and 20 degrees West, and we intended to approach the Pole between these meridians, flying in northerly and then southerly directions. Of course, it was necessary to have the sun clearly visible throughout much of the flight, so that we could use the astro compass and the sextant. We also needed clear weather beneath us, so that we could take drift readings on the ice.

During the morning, barometric pressure readings became more favourable. The fog dispersed, and the meteorological officer was able to give us a good forecast for Akureyri 30 hours later. Tim was presented with the problem of deciding whether to take off at a rather unfavourable time or abandon the attempt, since the time allotted to us did not permit further waiting. There was only one answer: he decided to take off.

Problems followed us to the aircraft. The repeater units of the distant-reading compass were found to be out of synchronisation; although these could be adjusted, experience had shown that such faults often recurred during flight. Other minor problems were sorted out and we were finally airborne, at 13.32 hours on 22 August 1942. Course was set from the mouth of the fjord on a track of 000 degrees and at a height of 50 feet, climbing slowly to 100 feet to conserve fuel. A voice was heard to whisper over the intercom:

'North Pole, here we come!'

From the start, the flight engineers kept the fuel consumption down to its lowest possible level, even though this meant flying at a true airspeed of less than 100 knots. The wind was from the north, while the sea was flat calm. By 15.39 hours, we had climbed slowly to 2,000 feet and levelled out. Visibility was clear, with 7/10ths alto-cumulus cloud ahead. The coast of Greenland could be seen far away to the west but we kept to our northern track and allowed the coastline to curve towards us later along that track, at about 75 degrees North. The compasses were checked by the astro compass and found to be correct, verifying that we were using the correct magnetic variation.

The first signs of drift ice appeared at about 16.30 hours, and Sandy began the routine of moving to and from the blisters from the navigation table, marking in green ink on the chart the position of the ice edge. To the east of Scoresby Sound, about a fifth of the sea was covered with ice. The floes varied from 20 to 200 feet in diameter, with the ice edge swinging north-eastwards in the direction of Jan Mayen Island.

By 17.50 hours, 'P for Peter' was flying over a large lead of open water, some 50 miles wide, to the east of Traill Island and Franz Josef Fjord. Twenty minutes later, the sea was strewn with drift ice, as our track converged with the coast of Greenland. At this stage of the journey, map-reading was very easy and the two pilots reported our position regularly.

At about 18.40 hours, we were able to check the variation setting on the magnetic compasses by using the astro compass; the variation of 30 degrees was found to be correct. Unfortunately, alto-cumulus cloud was by then covering 9/10ths of the sky, and the prospects of suitable weather conditions for a polar flight began to look far less favourable. The wind speed increased to 20 knots, from due north.

Even worse, we could see thick fog ahead of us, enveloping the islands along the coastline and stretching 40 miles out to sea, where it reached down to the surface.

Sandy came back to mark heavy pack ice on the chart. By the time he returned to the blisters, the Catalina had entered thick fog.

There seemed no hope of finding clearer conditions at sea level. The only possible solution was to try to climb above it, which was an unusual experience for us. Fifteen minutes later, the aircraft was still in thick cloud, with the temperature dropping to below freezing point and everyone watching for icing. A continuous radar check was kept on the coastline, and the pilots managed to 'map-read' by radar, keeping a close eye on their copy of the Admiralty chart and frequently changing direction to stay away from the land. I kept watch on my compass repeater unit and plotted these changes of course, also taking frequent peeps at the radar screen. There was a dim blur from the sun for a few moments, and we were able to make another check on the accuracy of our compass course.

At 22.05 hours, when we were to the east of the Franske Islands, there was an improvement in downward visibility and we were able to check the wind velocity by the drift method. But we soon had to climb again. The temperature dropped to minus five degrees when we reached 6,400 feet, the highest that 'P for Peter' had ever flown. There was still no sign of clearance.

We were approaching the 80th parallel, the point at which normal navigation methods would have to be replaced by the polar techniques which we had devised with the aid of Professor Debenham at Cambridge University. This would require intense concentration by the pilots and myself. The primary requirement now was good weather. The sun had to be clearly visible and cloud conditions had to favour continuing sunshine for the next twelve hours. There had to be no fog to mar our view of the ice beneath the aircraft. It was necessary to cruise with the minimum rate of fuel consumption throughout the flight, if we were to be able to return to Akureyri. We were still not absolutely certain that weather conditions would be good when we reached Iceland, and that we would not have to waste the last precious drops fuel in hunting for the entrance of Eyja Fjord.

Tim came back to the navigation compartment for a short conference with Sandy and myself. He already knew Ronnie's opinion. Our endurance had been shortened by all the climbing. There was no sign of any clearance. The basic requirement of clear visibility could not be satisfied. It would have been foolhardy to risk heavy icing, with the prospect of further deterioration, as midnight approached. There was no alternative but to descend once more, turn about, and head for Akureyri.

We abandoned the attempt at 22.31 hours, in position 79 degrees 11 minutes North, 15 degrees West. We had not even crossed the 80th parallel. All our researches into polar navigation had to remain just a theoretical exercise. We were all disappointed, but common sense had to prevail.

The northern headland of Ile de France was sighted about 45 minutes later. From there onwards, progress was mainly by map-reading. However, there were still many records to be kept, in addition to the usual entries in the navigation log. Sandy continued his analysis of the ice conditions along the coast of Greenland. Tim and Ronnie continued to write up the record that Sandy wanted of wet and dry bulb thermometer readings; the thermometer had been lashed to the barrel of the Vickers gun, which was pointing upwards from the front turret, and they used binoculars to take the readings through the windscreen. After midnight, I had some long sessions in the starboard blister, taking photographs of the Greenland coastline in very dim light. We were all trying to recoup something from our disappointing flight, hoping that our efforts might be of some use to someone in the future.

Our Catalina continued to progress smoothly until 02.40 hours, when we were flying at 1,800 feet with a thin layer of fog shrouding scattered ice floes below. The peaceful serenity was shattered by a sudden cough from the starboard engine. This had never happened before and we all jerked or reeled forward as the airspeed suddenly dropped. The crew put the emergency drill into effect and prepared for a forced landing. This was a most unpleasant prospect when flying over drift ice. My immediate job was to feed the wireless operator with accurate summaries of the aircraft's track and position; this was quite easy since we were off Cape Gladstone and heading for Scoresby Sound, which provided a safe haven for an emergency landing.

Fortunately, Catalinas were capable of flying on one engine when not excessively laden. No one knew what was wrong with the starboard engine but, whatever it was, there was the worry that the port engine would follow suit. Incandescent gases from the faulty engine seemed to signify incomplete combustion. But the port engine continued to run sweetly.

When Scoresby Sound was reached at 03.18 hours, another decision had to be taken. Should we send a final position signal, make a forced landing in the sheltered waters of the Sound and await some form of rescue, or should we risk the crossing over the open sea to Iceland? Tim had faith in 'P for Peter' and kept the starboard engine at quarter throttle, the point just below which it started to cough. He still had the duty of delivering Sandy to Spitsbergen. We headed for Akureyri, but kept the dinghies at the ready.

The last vestiges of drift ice disappeared at 04.00 hours and, although we had to descend to 700 feet to keep visual contact with the surface of the sea through the fog, the Icelandic coast proved to be clear. The meteorological officer had been a master of his craft.

We all breathed sighs of relief when safely moored at 06.40 hours, after having been airborne for over 17 hours. For once, we had not achieved our objective. Some of the crew thought that the fates had been unkind to us, but I preferred to think that we had been very fortunate. If we had not been compelled to turn back when we did, the engine would probably have started giving trouble at 85 degrees North, over solid pack ice. The outcome then could have been extremely serious.

Tim showed no signs of distress at our bad luck, and confined his observations to a characteristically humorous comment: 'If our distress signal had given our position at 85 degrees North, RAF HQ Iceland wouldn't have believed it! Just imagine the fun there would have been over the air waves!'

The first job was to notify the various authorities that we had been forced to abandon the 'northern flight' and that we could not carry out our part in Operation Gearbox on 24 August. Our two flight engineers worked long hours on the engine, in difficult conditions while the aircraft was tossing at its moorings, but they could not find the cause of the trouble. The tanks were emptied and refilled with fresh fuel, without finding any trace of the water that had been suspected. When the engines were started, they turned perfectly. Test flights were carried out and, again, there was no sign of anything wrong.

The engineers were thus in a quandary. One of them, David Baird, was convinced that the engine was 'jinxed' and getting its own back on us for having been forced to operate on excessively lean mixtures. For the first time since the beginning of our Arctic operations, morale began to sag. Tim's attitude was that, since the test flights had proved satisfactory, he expected to fly to Spitsbergen on 25 August. Nevertheless, he was well aware of the tension in his crew and, on the evening of 24 August, sent Ronnie round to the sergeants' mess to find out what they really thought. Ronnie came back with a simple message:

'They are all willing to go if you want to do so, but the married men are going to write farewell letters to their wives, just in case we do attempt to fly to Spitsbergen.'

That settled it. Tim signalled for permission to return to Sullom Voe and for the flight for Spitsbergen to be started from there after the engine had been properly checked.

The return flight to our home base began at 08.15 hours on 27 August. 'P for Peter' had never before carried such a despondent crew. There was none of the usual enthusiasm, faces were miserable and there was not even any conversation. The sergeants felt that they had let Tim down and caused him to fail in a mission.

Halfway home, the starboard engine suddenly coughed and lost power, exactly as before. The effect on the sergeants was electrifying and even hilarious. There were triumphant whoops of joy from all directions. The men had been proved correct and were entirely vindicated. David Baird swore at his charge and dared it to fall off the wing. The fact that we might find ourselves in the drink seemed of no significance. Ronnie made sure that the emergency procedures were carried out, and I passed a flow of position signals to the wireless operators. Tim just smiled ruefully, in the knowledge that his decision had been correct, even if he had been influenced by the sergeants. We wondered what Sandy thought of this strange display of RAF emotion.

The port engine carried the extra strain once more and, on reaching Sullom Voe, Tim brought the Catalina down on the water with his customary skill. The station engineering staff began work on her immediately, but their efforts were no more revealing than those of our own crew. The engine worked perfectly during the subsequent test flight and 'P for Peter' was passed as fit for service. But Tim insisted that something was wrong with the aircraft and he was backed both by our squadron commander and Coastal Command Headquarters. The Catalina was flown to Gourock for the engine to be stripped down until the fault was discovered.

In due course, we learned the answer. David Baird had been right. The engine had been reacting to its maltreatment. Persistent running on lean mixtures had scorched the valve headings. Both engines had been affected. The scorches had become packed with carbon. On the starboard engine, the carbon had cracked when under heavy load, possibly when we were climbling to 6,400 feet, but had sealed up again when the engine cooled down. It was only the carbon in the port engine which had, on two occasions, brought us back to safety.

Many years later, I learned that our flights had given rise to recommendations for two unusual awards. Sir Philip Joubert was so impressed by the team work on these long Arctic flights that he tried to get the Polar Medal for all of us. But the scientific results and the hardships involved were not considered to equate with those of the land expeditions which had previously resulted in the granting of such awards. The Norwegians also wished to make some awards, but the RAF preferred these to be restricted to the Norwegian War Cross for our captain and the Norwegian War Medal for Sergeant T.R. Thomas.

Fate had decreed that 'P for Peter' could not take Sandy back to Spitsbergen as originally planned. Nor could any other Catalina, for the weather closed down at Sullom Voe. By the time it had cleared, it was time for 210 Squadron to send a large detachment to North Russia. Although it was suggested that Sandy could be taken in a Catalina en route to Russia, an alternative arrangement was made to fly him back to Iceland to complete his journey in one of the cruisers which were ordered to carry further reinforcements to Barentsberg.

That operation code-named 'Gearbox 2' was as successful as its predecessor. The cruisers *Cumberland* and *Sheffield* arrived at the Green Harbour fjord on successive days, both being attended by the destroyer *Eclipse*. Once again, Vice-Admiral Stuart S. Bonham-Carter was in charge of the operation. *Cumberland* reached Spitsbergen on 17 September, carrying more Norwegian troops under the command of Lieutenant-Colonel Tornerud, who was to take command of the garrison while Captain Ullring reported back to London. The cruiser also carried 130 tons of equipment and some Huskie dogs. The stores were unloaded within six hours, while the cruiser's crew remained continuously at action stations. On the next day, *Sheffield* unloaded 110 tons of supplies.

The heaviest equipment included three 40 mm Bofors guns and two Fordson tractors, all five items weighing over two tons each. These were hauled ashore on an improvised raft, crude in design but effective in use, supported by twenty 50 gallon drums.

Captain Ullring went aboard both cruisers to give an account of enemy activities and his own actions during the previous six weeks.

Early in August, he had taken the motor cutter and nine men northwards along the west coast to Kingsfjord in search of a German meteorological station. He found a recent footprint, but no sign of the enemy. On 20 August, a U-boat had visited Icefjord, Green Harbour and Advent Bay, and had bombarded several places. The Norwegians had returned fire with a Colt in the motor cutter alongside the quay at Barentsberg and with an Oerlikon on the hill slope above the township. The U-boat withdrew to use its 4 inch shells from a greater range, but had caused no casualties.

Captain A.W. Clarke of *Sheffield* was so impressed by Ullring's exploits in 'carrying on attacks on a U-boat from a rowing boat armed with a tin opener', to use the words of his official report, that he sent ashore two depth charges to augment the armoury of the Norwegians.

On completion of the two-day operation, Glen and Ullring remained ashore, the former to complete his duties in connection with the *Gearbox 2* operation, and the latter to hand over command to Tornerud. They knew that arrangements had been made by Coastal Command for Tim Healy to call with 'P for Peter' at Barentsberg a week later, on the way back from North Russia. Meanwhile, Major Whatman was destined to stay at Barentsberg throughout the winter of 1942/3, acting as British Liaison Officer.

CHAPTER ELEVEN

Operation Orator

During the passage of convoy PQ17, the movement of German battleships to the most northerly Norwegian fjords had indicated that their selected point of attack was likely to be to the east of Bear Island and that they did not fear an engagement with Allied capital ships so close to their line of retreat. Certainly the British Commander-in-Chief had been reluctant to allow his battle-fleet to operate in the Barents Sea, where there was a greater risk from U-boats and torpedo bombers. More positive measures were needed to protect convoy PQ18 in the Barents Sea, where its predecessor had received its heaviest mauling.

Several steps were taken to deter the German commander from sending his heavy units against the convoy. The merchant vessels were provided with a stronger screen of destroyers as close escorts, although this was at the expense of the protection of the Home Fleet. The carrier *Avenger* was included in the escort, with a complement of twelve Hurricanes and three Swordfish. The Allied covering force of battleships was to be at readiness to the west of Bear Island, but it could be brought into action only if there was reliable information about the deployment of the German heavy warships.

The part of the RAF in these preparations was code-named Operation Orator, and it was carried out wholly by Coastal Command. The detachments were under the command of Group Captain F.R. Hopps, who set up his headquarters at Polyarnoe, a Russian naval base on the western side of the Kola Inlet, on the north coast of Russian Lapland. He commanded a mixed force of Hampdens, Spitfires and Catalinas.

The first difficulty that the planners in Coastal Command had to overcome was the movement of aircraft and equipment to North Russia. The journey was well within the range of the Catalina flying boats but the landplanes were stretched to the limits of their endurances. The 'safe' range of a Hampden, without torpedo and without overload tanks, was considered to be no more than 1,040 nautical miles. If it flew at a steady 125 knots and did not have to use

191

rich mixture for manoeuvring or climbing, its absolute maximum range to 'dry tanks' might be extended to 1,360 miles, but this was not with any confidence. A safe route from Sumburgh, the most northerly aerodrome in the Shetlands, to Vaenga, from where they were to operate in North Russia, was 1,314 miles. This route would have kept the Hampdens at least 60 miles from enemy territory at all times, but it was obviously impracticable. A route following the coastline would have covered 1,200 miles, but this was considered far too dangerous. A more direct route over the mountains of Norway involved a flight of over 1,100 miles, but so much fuel was likely to be consumed in climbing over the mountains that there would be little margin for contingencies such as head winds, engine troubles, navigational errors or delays in landing.

Two squadrons of Hampdens, 144 and 455, were detached from their base at Leuchars in Fife for the enterprise. It was realised that the despatch of 32 aircraft on such a flight was extremely hazardous, but such was the importance of convoy PQ18 that the risks had to be taken. Permission was received from the Russians to make use of the aerodromes at Afrikanda, Beloe and Gremiakha, near the town of Kandalaksha, on the gulf of that name at the south-west extremity of the White Sea. These aerodromes had the advantages of being a little nearer than Vaenga, of being more easily recognisable, and of having less likelihood of an air raid alert when the Hampdens arrived. The route was at sea level to approximately 65 degrees North 07 degrees East, then turning to follow a direct line to Kandalaksha, crossing the Norwegian coastline at about 66 degrees North. The crews hoped to fly over the Norwegian mountains during darkness and to pick up the Kandalaksha to Murmansk railway at the end of the flight. They would have to fly over Swedish and Finnish territory, but any repercussions from this would have to be accepted.

Sixteen Hampdens from each squadron left Sumburgh on the evening of 4 September 1942. There were fears at Coastal Command Headquarters about the number which would reach their destination, for there had been insufficient time to acquire and fit long-range tanks. In the event, 23 of the 32 aircraft made safe landings at Afrikanda or other Russian aerodromes. Two more reached Russia but ran out of fuel. One of these made a 'wheels up' landing in a soft and mossy field at Khibini, not far from its destination, and was slightly damaged. The other force-landed on some tree stumps and became a total loss. Both crews were unhurt. A third Hampden had

A typical example of drift ice, covering about 9/10th of the sea.

The wreckage of a Hampden being transported by barge near Vadsø in northern Norway. Research by an ex-navigator on Hampdens, Harry R. Moyle, indicates that this is AT109 letter C of 455 (Australia) Squadron, flown by Squadron Leader Jimmy Catanach, DFC. The machine was hit by *Ubootjäger 1105* and made a crash landing, all five men in the crew being taken PoW.

the misfortune to be shot down by Russian fighters at the mouth of the Kola Inlet, one of the crew being killed; there was an air raid in progress at the time, and the Russians did not recognise the Hampden, which was flying outside the prescribed air corridor.

Of the remaining six Hampdens, three were shot down by fighters over Finland or near its border, some of the men surviving to become PoWs. Another was shot down by a German patrol boat over the coast of Norway, and all the men became PoWs. Two crashed in Sweden, and in one of these all the men were killed. The other was found 34 years later at 5,000 feet on the side of Tsatsa mountain, in a remote part of Sweden about fifteen miles north of the intended track. The pilot and a passenger, a signals corporal, escaped with slight injuries, but the remaining men were killed. The two survivors had to scramble over the mountains for three days before finding a village.*

The Hampdens which reached Russia were armed with Mark XII torpedoes, which had been carried in the cruiser USS *Tuscaloosa*, together with most of the ground crews. None of these aircraft saw combat while in Russia, but it is probable that their presence had a deterrent effect on German plans. They took part in only one mission, a pre-emptive patrol on 14 September. A reconnaissance over Narvik showed that *Tirpitz* was not there, and the battleship could not be located. This was at the time when convoy PQ18 was in a particularly vulnerable position. Group Captain Hopps sent out all 23 aircraft on a 'reconnaissance in force'. They flew to the farthest position that *Tirpitz* could have reached and then turned back on its probable track, as far as the Catalina patrol area. Nothing was seen and all the aircraft returned safely, after a flight of 7½ hours. An afternoon flight found *Tirpitz* back in Narvik; she had merely been out for sea trials.

For most of the time, the Hampdens remained dispersed on Vaenga aerodrome, but they suffered some damage from air raids. When the time came to return to the UK, in mid-October, the aircrews joined the ground crews in the warship, while their torpedo bombers were handed over to the Russians. The long return flight, against the prevailing wind, was regarded by Headquarters of Coastal Command as too hazardous.

---

*The fate of these Hampdens and their crews has been exhaustively examined by an ex-navigator of 44 Squadron, Harry R. Moyle, as part of his book *The Hampden File*, in preparation.

A small force of Spitfires was required in North Russia for reconnaissance purposes. The maximum radius of action of this machine, when fitted with long-range tanks, was only as far as Trondheim fjord from the UK. The other aircraft of Coastal Command's Photographic Reconnaissance Unit (PRU) was the Mosquito IV. This could reach Narvik when fitted with 50 gallon drop-tanks, but not Altenfjord. Thus three Spitfire IVs were detached from 1 PRU at Benson and flew via Sumburgh on 1 September, following the same route as that planned for the Hampdens three days later. They all arrived safely at Afrikanda, their flight averaging 4½ hours. The ground crews travelled on the USS *Tuscaloosa*.

From Afrikanda, the three Spitfires flew to Vaenga, where the roundels on their duck-egg blue camouflage were replaced with red Russian stars. Using their vertical and oblique F24 cameras, the pilots flew twelve sorties over Narvik and Altenfjord, bringing back regular reports of the enemy warships. One Spitfire was badly damaged in an air raid, and a replacement was flown out on 16 September. The enemy warships were inactive, apart from the occasion when *Tirpitz* went out on sea trials. One of the Spitfires was lost on a low-level sortie over Altenfjord on 27 September, probably as the result of ground fire, and the pilot was killed.

When their duties were finished, the pilots handed over the three remaining Spitfires to the Russians, who were very anxious to acquire them. Then they and the ground crews joined the Hampden squadron men on the return journey by warship.

The third contribution made by Coastal Command towards Operation Orator was the dual function provided by the Catalinas of 210 Squadron. At the beginning and the end of the route of convoy PQ18, our main task was to provide a close anti-submarine escort. When operating from Russia, the Catalinas were fitted with overload tanks and could not also carry depth charges; their function was to menace the U-boats and inform the warships of their presence, rather than to attack. The Catalinas flying from Sullom Voe or from Iceland, without overload tanks, did carry depth charges. On 23 September 1942, Flight Sergeant J.W. Semmens of 210 Squadron, flying from Sullom Voe in Catalina 'U', attacked and sank *U-253* about 115 miles to the north of Cape Langanaes in Iceland. The U-boat, which had left Kiel on 12 September on its first war cruise, was sighted on the surface less than a mile away. It crash-dived, but Semmens straddled the swirl with six 250 lb depth

OPERATIONS IN NORTH RUSSIA

charges. In an upheaval of water, the U-boat came to the surface on its side. It sank but then rose again. Then it rolled over and disappeared, with the stern almost vertical. The captain, Kapitän-leutnant A. Friedrichs, and the entire crew of about 40 lost their lives.

The other function of our Catalinas was even more important. This was to maintain ten 'cross-over' patrols against surface vessels. These patrols were designated AA to KK and, on a chart, looked like straight-sided figures of eight. They were designed to ensure that no enemy battleship could pass through the patrol area without being picked up by airborne radar. Thus the Commander-in-Chief could be informed of any enemy warships which might approach the convoy. The centre line of the patrols ran from 69 degrees North 10 degrees East to 71 degrees North 36 degrees East, about 100 miles from the Norwegian coastline. The patrol areas moved north-eastwards as the convoy moved slowly past North Cape of Norway. The southerly patrols, AA to CC, were carried out by Catalinas which operated solely from Sullom Voe. For the central patrols, DD and EE, the Catalinas took off from Sullom Voe but flew on to Russia after completing the required number of circuits. Patrol EE was the most difficult, since it was the farthest from either base, and the aircraft could remain on station for only a short time; five Catalinas were required in succession to ensure that a continuous watch was maintained. The northerly patrols, FF to KK, were carried out solely from Russia.

On the outward flight the Catalinas might not make their first landfall until sixteen hours after leaving the Shetlands. Low stratus cloud usually prevented the use of astro sights, so that accurate dead-reckoning was essential if the tracks were to be kept within the scheduled turning points. Those who planned the operation must have had confidence in the ability of 210 Squadron to provide such a service.

It was originally intended that, while in Russia, the Catalinas should be based at Lake Lakhta, a fresh water lake a few miles to the south-west of Archangel, on the southernmost tip of the White Sea. Grasnaya, on the Kola Inlet, was available as an advanced base. However, Group Captain Hopps soon discovered that communications between the Kola Inlet and Lake Lakhta were so poor that it was necessary to make greater use of Grasnaya. This was 400 miles nearer the patrol areas but suffered from the disadvantage of being nearer to enemy-occupied Norway. In fact, Lakhta was used as a rest camp and also as a base for the close escort duties carried out by the Catalinas during the final stages of the passage of convoy PQ18.

Nine Catalinas operated from the Russian bases during Operation Orator. Each left Sullom Voe in a carefully planned sequence. In Tim Healy's Catalina, we were the eighth to depart. For us, the operation had brought a change of impetus and motivation, as well as some alterations in personal relationships. Although all our squadron crews were still 'on their own' as they faced the elements over the vast expanses of Arctic seas, we no longer had the feeling of complete isolation that we had experienced on the ice reconnaissances and the attempt to reach the North Pole.

Tim had been carrying a heavy load of personal responsibility during four months of intensive flying, and the resulting operational weariness had been intensified by the disappointment of not having crossed the 80th parallel, on the flight that was to have been our greatest achievement. But there was a bright light welcoming him forward to one more month of hard work. At the end of Operation Orator, Tim would have completed the 1,000 hours of flying which marked the end of a first operational tour in Catalinas. He was looking forward to a change of duties, and to be with his family again.

A combination of other factors also contributed to the feeling that things were now different for us. Since 'P for Peter' was still unserviceable, Tim had now taken over 'S for Sugar'. This was a good aircraft, with all the standard fittings for operational flying, but it did not have the special trimmings to which we had become accustomed on 'P for Peter'.

Even more important were the changes in the crew. Ronnie Martin's promotion to captaincy could no longer be delayed. He departed to take charge of Catalina 'T for Tommy'. His replacement was Flying Officer Reginald W. Witherick, a newcomer to the squadron. Reg had suffered the misfortune of losing his left hand in an accident with a propeller blade, shortly before joining the squadron. He had a set of attachments for his wrist which enabled him to fly the aircraft from the second pilot's seat, and did so with such remarkable competence that no one had any qualms when he was at the controls.

Sergeant Kingett and Sergeant Campbell had both completed 1,000 hours of operational flying and were transferred to other duties. Sergeant R. Isaacs and Leading Aircraftman T. Carter took their places, while Sergeant T.R. Thomas was elevated to fill the post of first wireless operator. I had been promoted to flight lieutenant

(*Right*) Flying Officer
Reginald W. Witherick.

(*Below*) Pilot Officer
George W. Adamson.

and another newcomer to the squadron, Pilot Officer George W. Adamson, joined the crew as second navigator and to augment the availability of qualified navigators while the squadron was in North Russia.

Such changes in crew membership were not uncommon, as personnel were moved to gain maximum benefit from everyone's experience, but they called for adjustments as the new members settled in. There was no time available for crew training; the newcomers had to adapt themselves to crew procedures as the flights progressed.

We took off at 11.30 hours on 12 September, to be the third aircraft on the central patrol EE. As we drew near to the Arctic Circle, a Blohm und Voss Ha 140 floatplane came within 800 yards of us, but turned away towards Trondheim without offering combat. It took over six hours to reach the most southerly point of the patrol area, and nearly three hours to make each complete circuit. On reaching the eastern extremity of the area, Tim flew eastwards for 50 miles to check that the weather was clear enough to permit a safe passage to the White Sea. We deepened our patrol slightly on our return, to compensate for the short absence. Everyone was on constant alert and a continuous radar watch was maintained, but nothing was sighted. Following the uneventful patrol, we landed at Lake Lakhta, having been in the air for 24 hours.

Viewed from the air in September 1942, the Arctic tundra was the wildest and most inhospitable place that we could imagine. It was a vast expanse of uninhabited rock, pool, marsh and bog, and a most undesirable place in which to have to make a forced landing. By contrast, Lake Lakhta presented a beautiful and welcoming picture, quietly secluded in the surrounding woodland with wisps of morning mist lying in patches over the placid water. It was a seaplane base for the Russian Naval Air Service but, as we landed, only our own Catalinas could be seen lying at the moorings. An efficient dinghy service, manned by a beaming Russian coxswain, took us ashore, where an interpeter was waiting to guide us along a 'roadway' made of tree trunks to our accommodation.

We were led to a hillside above the lake, where there was a two-storey building made of brick and wood, very much in need of paint and maintenance. Two flanking statues of a young man and a young woman, in culture poses and also in need of renovation, gave the impression that it must have been a workers' hostel at some time, perhaps the Russian equivalent of the German 'Strength through

Joy' movement. Our quarters were on the first floor, in a large dormitory with beds packed close together. Sheets and blankets were provided, and the room was heated by large wood-burning stoves. There was a separate mess room, the tables covered with oilcloth, with pictures of Lenin and Stalin keeping watch on our activities. The sanitary arrangements were crude but effective, a twin-seater over a long drop which we dubbed the 'fifty-footer'. It was on the north side of the building, and the wind blows cold in those parts.

The food was not to everyone's taste, but they made plentiful use of vegetables and dried fruit. I found the *tchi* (tea) quite refreshing, although it was sweet and syrupy, but I avoided the over-generous helpings of vodka. In due course, supplies of our own tinned rations caught up with us. These improved the diet, and the flying rations were especially welcome. Clearly, our Russian hosts could spare few resources for the comforts of life. They had to make do with whatever was available, but they gave us the best they could. Certainly they made up for any material deficiencies with the warmth of their hospitality and their spirit of co-operation.

The Russian engineering technicians were very competent. With wartime shortages of equipment, they had to 'make do and mend', and were eager to demonstrate their skill at so doing. Powers of improvisation, coupled with a capacity for hard work, seemed to be the main attributes of their maintenance system. They checked a petrol leak in a Catalina, which our men had failed to stop. They cheerfully undertook to repair the Hampden which had made a belly landing. A Catalina which had been shot up by an enemy aircraft was brought up the slipway at Grasnaya within eight minutes of arrival, and the subsequent repairs were efficiently completed. Once a job was begun, the men went on working until it was finished. If at times they were slow in starting, they made up for this deficiency in their staying-power.

George Adamson, who was an artist by profession, later wrote a diary and described life at Lake Lakhta in these terms:

> It was really lively during those groups of two or three days when we would be based at Lakhta – with most of the squadron there and Wing Commander Johnson, a cheery 'Whizzo' commanding officer. The long pale blue dormitory upstairs would ring with noise – poker dice games, chopping wood for the huge wall stoves, gin and vodka parties; and tired crews would come in and sleep, careless of the din.

At nights it was funny . . the lights would rise and dim like the Northern Lights. The story spread around of poor slaves pedalling to drive the dynamos . . . and cries of 'crack the whip' greeted each fall in the lighting. The 'fifty-footer' too, now a little improved by the generous application of Jeyes Fluid, brought its fund of laughter – the updraught was strong sometimes, and paper light. I recall the scene every morning of an old woman, she must have been nearly seventy, who carried buckets of water up the steep slope from the lake to the house, then upstairs to their place of readiness outside the washplace. She used to trudge about, her head wrapped peasant-wise with a checked kerchief – muttering to herself as she swept the (awful) mess on the floor of our room – or tidied our beds. Women in Russia do a lot of hard manual labour – and many look unfemininely able at that! It used to rankle us able-bodied youths sitting on our beds whilst 'Belinda' skivvied.

We were up early on 15 September and left Lake Lakhta at 06.10 hours GMT (09.10 hours local time) for a five-hour transit flight to Grasnaya. We refuelled and set off again at 15.25 hours GMT (17.25 hours local time), in order to carry out two operational tasks. The first was to fly along the coastline of Novaya Zemlya to see whether there were any casualties from the convoy in need of assistance. It so happened that only one ship was lost on that stage of the convoy's passage, and there was nothing to report.

The second duty was to provide a close anti-submarine escort for the convoy. It was on this flight that Tim had his only experience of sighting a U-boat on the surface. Visibility was less than half a mile when it was spotted. Of course, the U-boat crash-dived, but the conning tower was still visible when we passed overhead. The German submariners must have had a fright, but they were in no danger from us. We carried overload tanks instead of depth charges, and our only offensive weapons were machine guns, which were unlikely to do much harm. Messages were passed to the nearest surface escorts and we cruised overhead to discourage the enemy, while the convoy passed by a few miles away. On returning to Grasnaya, our records showed that we had been flying for 28 of the previous 32 hours.

All the captains in our squadron were impressed with the efficiency of the Russian marinecraftmen at Grasnaya. Elsewhere, when approaching a buoy, it was the invariable practice not to switch off engines until safely moored. The procedure at Grasnaya was different. A dinghy, manned by one coxswain, came well out and the Catalina engines were switched off at his signal. When the propellers had stopped rotating, he approached the aircraft and threw a heaving line, which was caught by the aircraft rigger. The rigger hauled in the line and looped the attached hawser over the bow bollard. The dinghy then towed the flying boat towards the shore and eventually turned sharply to starboard, so that the aircraft approached the slipway from a direction parallel with the shoreline.

Meanwhile, two of the Catalina's crew had mounted on to the starboard wing-tip. The dinghy again turned sharply to starboard, so that the port float was lifted high over the slipway, followed by the aircraft's tail. As the tail passed overhead, a Russian who was standing on the slipway with a hooked line caught the hook in the towing aperture underneath it. The other end of the towing line was attached to a tractor, with engine running, at the head of the slipway. The Catalina was held steady in the water by the slipway, with the tractor and dinghy pulling in opposite directions. Two more Russians in rubber suits floated out and attached the beaching wheels. Then the dinghy's hawser was cast off, while the tractor hauled the aircraft up the slipway. Ten minutes after alighting on the water, the Catalina was parked close to the towering cliffs of the Kola Inlet, safe from air attack. It was excellent teamwork, success depending mainly on the accuracy of the man with the hooked line on the slipway. When the interpreter was asked what would happen if he missed the hole, he replied rather ominously: 'He *never* misses!'

On the morning of 18 September, we were off again for more close escort duties and reached the convoy at 13.12 hours, when it was entering the White Sea. The Senior Naval Officer with the convoy was told of two stray merchant vessels just to the north of Cape Kanin. We exchanged signals with a Catalina that had been awaiting our arrival before returning to base. Then began the steady circuiting of the convoy. Russian aircraft were also taking part, giving us extra cause for alertness. In poor visibility, mistaken identity could be very costly.

The wind was light and the sky was clear. As evening approached, a bank of fog settled over the White Sea. We did not relish the prospect of hunting for the air corridor in darkness and fog, over forest and tundra, when we made our return journey. The safest course was to return to Cape Kanin and stooge up and down the Barents Sea until dawn. This meant extending a 15-hour flight to 24 hours, but the Catalina carried enough fuel for such an eventuality.

Sea fog at night gave us no opportunity for drift taking, but the cloudless sky brought ideal conditions for astro observations, apart from the cold. The night was spent in flying one-hourly legs in northerly and southerly directions, taking three-star fixes on each leg. It was a busy night in the navigation compartment. Others contributed by keeping out of the way and supplying hot drinks. As dawn approached, we made our way back to the coast, en route for Lake Lakhta.

It was at such times that weariness could give rise to errors of judgment. The safest procedure would have been to head for a landfall to the east of Cape Kanin and then coast-crawl westwards. I must have been over-confident in the quality of the astro fixes, for I headed straight for Cape Kanin. All would have been well if there had been good visibility, but the pilots could see for only 400 yards. Even excellent astro could not satisfy that degree of accuracy.

On reaching land, Tim had to make a quick decision. He thought we were to the west, along the coast of Russian Lapland towards Murmansk, and turned east. I thought we had arrived at the coastline near Cape Kanin and that we should turn west to the entrance of the White Sea. Both these coastlines were similarly shaped and very desolate. Our maps and charts were not very helpful and, in poor visibility, one stretch of Arctic tundra looks very much like another.

We followed the coastline to the south-east and eventually it turned westwards. This confirmed my belief that we had arrived at Cheshskaya Bay and that our best course of action would be to fly westwards over the narrow isthmus of the Kanin peninsula to regain the White Sea. Tim was not so confident. He did not favour flying over land which might lead us to the higher ground of Russian Lapland. Within a few minutes, however, his worries disappeared as a broad expanse of ocean appeared before us, verifying my belief. Thankful to be flying again over water, we turned southwards towards Archangel. It was still foggy and the air corridor still had to be reached, but most of our problems seemed behind us.

A strident blast on the warning horn suddenly brought everyone to action stations. However, it was not enemy action which was the cause, but Tim's decision to land. He had seen that the coastline curved northwards and was worried about running short of fuel. At the same time, he had seen a coastal settlement, the first sign of civilisation since we had left the Kola Inlet. The front hatches and covers had to be closed and the wing-tip floats lowered. Tim scanned the surface of the water to ensure there was no floating timber, a common hazard in these parts, but he was very weary and did not check the direction of the wind. As soon as the Catalina lost forward momentum, one float dipped deeply into water and the aircraft swung round to head up wind. There had been no time to stow the crockery and half of it crashed into the bilges. On the next flight, someone would have to wait for his food.

We taxied towards the settlement to seek guidance, a Union Jack fluttering from one blister to signify our good intentions. As we lay offshore with the engines gently ticking over, a rowing boat came out. It was manned by a solitary figure in a peaked cap, dark green smock and knee-length boots. He looked like the local police officer, but he was a jovial character who was clearly in a friendly mood. We could speak no Russian and he knew no English. Members of the crew tried him with French, Italian, Spanish and even German, but nothing clicked. A map of the White Sea produced no response. Then I copied out in Cyrillic script the name of the settlement where I thought we were. I had been so confident about this that I had already written it laboriously on my chart. He beamed and pointed to the settlement; we were in the right place after all. At this moment, the fog started to clear and we could see farther. The unexpected swing of the coastline was no more than a bay, not marked on the map.

Our Russian friend was rewarded with a bar of chocolate and his boat was pushed away. We were soon airborne again for Lakhta. On arrival, Tim was commended for his wisdom in staying airborne, but there was no shortage of ribaldry about the final episode. It was a dubious distinction to become the only squadron navigator who had to stop and ask a policemen for the way home!

*

Convoy PQ18 was more successful than its predecessor. On 19 September, 27 of the original 40 merchant ships reached Archangel. The Luftwaffe, which had deployed 225 long-range bombers, torpedo bombers and dive bombers from Norway, sank ten of the remainder; they suffered heavy losses in the process, from AA fire and the Hurricanes launched from the aircraft carrier. But the U-boats sank only three ships, while they lost three of their own number from attacks by the escort vessels.

The convoy sailing in the reverse direction, QP14, left Archangel on 13 September. The fourteen merchant ships, mostly survivors of convoy PQ17, had the benefit of thick weather to protect them from aircraft as they approached North Cape, but there was still a toll of four merchant ships and two escort vessels before the convoy reached Iceland. In addition to the sinking of *U-253*, already mentioned, there was another attack made by a Catalina on a U-boat. This was 'Z for Zebra' of 330 (Norwegian) Squadron, based at Akureyri and captained by Lieutenant Stansburg. The crew sighted a U-boat on 21 September, when the convoy was to the north of Jan Mayen Island. Somewhat unusually, the U-boat remained on the surface to shoot it out, hitting the Catalina with 20 mm cannon fire and wounding two of the crew. Stansburg pressed home his attack with four depth charges, but apparently did not make a 'kill'. The Catalina was so badly damaged that Stansburg had to make a forced landing, the crew being picked up by the convoy's leading escort, the destroyer *Marne*.

Coastal Command's contribution to the protection of convoys PQ18 and QP14 had involved more than 100 aircraft from thirteen squadrons, based in the UK, Iceland and Russia. These flew 269 sorties, with 2,320 hours of flying time, although only 184½ hours were spent over the convoys. Almost half the sorties were made by Catalinas. Eight U-boats were sighted and two attacked. The heavy ships of the Kriegsmarine had not put to sea, and it is reasonable to assume that the aircraft based in North Russia had worried the German commander.

The part that Coastal Command had played in the Spitsbergen venture had also contributed indirectly to the relative success of convoy PQ18. The destroyer escorts could not complete their long journey to Russia without refuelling. In addition to the tankers which accompanied the convoy, tankers were stationed at Lowe Sound in Spitsbergen, so that some of the destroyers were able to break off and refuel before reaching the most hazardous part of their journey. Without the earlier reconnaissances and landings, this would not have been practicable.

The first week of the Russian detachment was the second occasion on which Tim and his crew had completed 70 hours flying in seven days. The other Catalina crews had been flying equally intensively. Everyone was in need of a rest, but first there was the long flight back to Sullom Voe. As the homeward trek started, with each aircraft taking an allocation of ground staff and equipment, there was a feeling of satisfaction that we had played our part in a well-planned operation.

CHAPTER TWELVE

Tragedy

On 21 September 1942, the Russian commander invited Wing Commander Johnson and two of his aircraft captains to a special dinner, to celebrate the friendship that had built up between our squadron and the local Russian forces. This was our last night at Lakhta. The hospitality was likely to be alcoholic and communication restricted to the formality of toasting each other. Our squadron commander took with him two of his most competent captains, Tim Healy and Jackie Holmes.

It was a cold evening, for the snow begins to fall in September in that sub-Arctic region. We kept the stoves burning brightly to welcome back our noble ambassadors. It seemed that international honours were evenly divided, but hangovers had been avoided, since we had to depart for Grasnaya early the following morning.

A month earlier, arrangements had been made for us to divert to Barentsberg on our way home from Russia, in order to pick up Sandy Glen and Captain Ullring. This flight had been planned for 23 September, but in the event weather forecasts were so bad that we had to bide our time. We could not tell the Russian 'met-lady' at Grasnaya of our diversion northwards, and had to interpret that part of her charts ourselves while her attention was concentrated on the southern route. Our regular visits to her office must have made her wonder why RAF airmen derived so much enjoyment from meteorology.

Our interpreter on these visits was Lieutenant Leo Trackenburg of the Russian Naval Service, whom we named 'George'. He was very hard-working and helpful, but had evidently learned his impeccable English at night school and was not familiar with meteorological jargon. A ridge of high pressure was described as a 'hill made up a lot of air', while a depression over the Barents Sea became a 'hole with nothing in it at all'. This caused a lot of laughter, in which the met-lady joined, especially when we asked whether anyone in the hole would be covered with snow. George was a friendly character and he served us well.

208

On the evening of 24 September, the forecast for the route to Sullom Voe was better. The weather chart for the northern part of our journey did not look equally favourable, but we could hope that Icefjord would be on the leeward side of the storms. Take-off was scheduled for 07.00 hours.

On our way back to our billets from the met office, Tim and I went down the steep side of Kola Inlet to the slipway, to make a final check that all was ready for the morrow. It was a dark night. Tim reminisced over the highlights and disappointments of the previous six months. He said that he hoped Ronnie Martin would be able to take over those crew members who still had some of their operational tour to complete, when we got back to Sullom Voe. Thus there would still be the nucleus for another attempt at the North Pole, if an opportunity should arise.

Tim was still keen to complete the job. For the first time with me, he talked about his family life and his hopes to be at home with Madeline when their second child was born. We discussed the strain that operational flying imposed on family life, and the courage that widows needed when good men like Dan Godfrey were never seen again. It could happen to any of us. We family men could only hope that our next-of-kin would have the strength of purpose to rebuild their lives and not agonise over what might have been. It was unusual for Tim to be so philosophical. The truth was that he was badly in need of a rest and a few home comforts.

There were some further changes on this homeward flight. Wing Commander Johnson had supervised the arrangements for all the Fritham and Gearbox flights, and he wanted to see for himself the scene of our activities. He flew with us as third pilot, but in fact occupied the second pilot's seat for much of the time. Tim wanted George Adamson to have some experience of Arctic navigation, so he was made responsible for the journey to Spitsbergen while I would take over for the journey from there to home.

On leaving the Kola Inlet, we flew round Kildin Island and then headed due north so as to avoid enemy-occupied Norway. We then turned north-west towards South Cape of Spitsbergen. The further north we flew, the more we realised that the met-lady's chart had been accurate. The sky was dark and heavily-laden, the sea was very rough, the wind increasingly blustery with gusts up 40 knots, and progress was slow. The chances of making a landing in Spitsbergen seemed slight. If we failed to land at Barentsberg we would have to return to Grasnaya, which would cause a delay of two days. Our squadron commander favoured an immediate return so that we could try again the next day. Tim agreed, and we turned around to follow the same route back to Grasnaya.

At 13.29 hours, when we were about 70 miles from the Russian coastline in position 70 degrees 11 minutes North 36 degrees 08 minutes East, the warning horn suddenly blared. My job in action was to act as gunnery control officer, since George Adamson was acting as first navigator. I grabbed my flying helmet and hurried aft to the blister compartment, to find out the cause of the alarm. A Ju88 was taking up position on the starboard quarter. Tim instructed the gunners to open fire as soon as the enemy came within range.

The Ju88 made his approach from about two miles away, about 500 feet above us at an angle of some 30 degrees. This gave the impression that the pilot intended to make a forward-firing attack on our starboard (green) quarter. Tim had no fears about air combat; there had been occasions when he had deliberately turned towards an unidentified aircraft in order to find out if it was an enemy.

When an attack was imminent, our crew drill was to maintain a steady course at first. This gave our gunners a steady platform from which to take aim. We delayed our own avoiding action until the enemy committed himself to an attacking line of approach. A sudden turn would then make it difficult for the enemy to allow correctly for the change in deflection.

The duty of the gunnery control officer was to tell the captain what was happening behind the Catalina, and to give instructions if there was a forward-firing attack from either of the rear quarters. He passed control to one of the pilots as soon as the enemy flew out of his field of vision. My running commentary went as follows:

'Green attack expected . . . range one mile . . . slightly up . . . stand by green turn . . . range half a mile . . . stand by green turn . . . rear attack off . . . passing on green beam . . . over to second pilot over. . . .'

The Ju88 pulled away from its feint attack and passed by us to our bow. As it did so, our starboard gunner opened fire. But the diving approach had increased the speed of the Junkers and our gunner made slightly insufficient allowance for deflection. Our .50 bullets could be seen hitting the rear part of the fuselage instead of the centre.

Our line of vision from the blister was blocked by the Catalina's mainplane as soon as the German aircraft passed by. Then there was a burst of gunfire from the enemy's rearward-firing MG15 7.92

machine guns. These sprayed along the hull of our flying boat, one armour-piercing bullet dropping at my feet, its force spent after passing through several bulkheads. During this fusillade, the Catalina had made a green turn, dipping sharply and then levelling out again.

The Ju88 continued to move away from us, to the south. I remained in the blister compartment, awaiting instructions to stand down. Our squadron commander was occupying the second pilot's seat. I had handed over to him, but had heard nothing over the intercom. After a couple of minutes, a crew member came aft to tell me that I was needed up front.

Throughout the encounter, George Adamson had been in the navigation compartment, able to hear but unable to see what was happening. He recorded the event afterwards in his diary:

The warning horn blurbed suddenly – for it's always sudden, that sound that puts us all at ready, and yet so often leads to nought. 'Give Tommy our position,' said Scho, and hurried aft with a helmet to do the fighting control. I did. We were about 70 nautical miles from the north coast of Russian Lapland. My job was done then, until the fighting was over.

There was the bark of gunfire and the metallic splutter of hits we were receiving. The pilot's cockpit was dulled with smoke; and little explosions like crack-a-jacks we watched there and in front of us . . . to stand is the only thing to do: and breathe a prayer. An impulse to duck passes with the realisation that it can do no good. I looked through the window over my table to see a glimpse of a Ju88 heading away at right angles to our track.

Tim was falling from his seat. I caught him heavily and pulled to keep his weight from the stick. The Winco called out. Two of us got him through the doorway and laid him huddled on the floorboard; unconscious, if not dead. I thought how futile it was, a fine lovable young man one moment, a helpless body the next. And I thought this is war. We gave Tim a charge of morphia, for what help it might have been, and laid him more comfortably, his head resting on my knees; and covered him with a sleeping bag in the hope that only shock and wounds were the trouble.

Fifty years later we learnt from Deutsche Dienststelle in Berlin that a Junkers Ju88 of the 1st Squadron of the Long Range Reconnaissance Group 22 based at Banak in Porsanger Fjord in Norway had crashed into the sea west of Tamsöy Island when returning from an Arctic operational flight. The four men in the crew were all killed. These were the pilot, Oberleutnant Joseph Hess, the air observer Oberleutnant Rolfgünter Bauer, the wireless operator Unteroffizier Herbert Winkler, and the air gunner Unteroffizier Karl Müller.

The day of the crash was 25 September 1942, the same day when our Catalina was attacked by a Ju88 over the Barents Sea. The cause of the crash was attributed to 'air combat with a Russian flying boat'. It was normal for Luftwaffe aircraft to report such incidents by radio as the action occurred, and thus the Staffel Headquarters at Banak would have been aware of the encounter. The German crew would have known that the Russians were operating Catalinas over the Barents Sea but not the RAF, in September 1942. In the heat of combat, they could easily have missed seeing the RAF roundels. In fact, our Catalina was the only one in that area on that day.

The Ju88 made a single diving attack on our aircraft. Both combatants scored hits on their adversaries. The enemy aircraft then broke off the engagement and continued its straight line flight southwards to the horizon and then Norway. The German burst of gunfire killed Flight Lieutenant Healy in the first pilot's seat and damaged several instruments as well as the aileron controls. This made level flying difficult so that we made a stall landing in the sea near the coast on the south of Killin Island. It is probable that the Ju88 received similar damage to its controls. The pilot would then have had to manoeuvre through fjords to Banak but crashed in doing so.

It was a remarkable achievement by our squadron commander to keep the Catalina on a steady course, without proper aileron control, steering partly by reference to wind lanes since he was unable to read the P9 compass. It was impossible to negotiate the sharp twists of the Kola Inlet, and the way he made our forced landing in the rough water near Kildin Island aroused the admiration of all in the crew. We were soon tied up to a Russian buoy. Once more, George Adamson's diary describes what happened:

'We sent another message and in a couple of hours, as dusk fell, we were all aboard a Russki submarine chaser, ploughing through the heavy coastal seas to Polyarnoe . . . and the [flying] boat secured to a buoy, stripped of her special apparatus [radar]. I shall not forget the two hours sail we had with decks awash, making angles of fifty degrees either way. We nearly all in turn got up on deck, for there at least the air was fresh and the movement seemed natural when its cause visible. We had to hang on for dear life. I remember . . . the sea with its phosphorescent bubbles and the pale glow of day against the rocky mountain skyline . . . and relief when we got in the inlet and on shore at Polyarnoe. At the Naval HQ we received every consideration and hospitality – warmth, rum, and a meal – and a bed. Our wet clothes were dried and everything was done so efficiently and naturally. Next day, after late breakfast, we were a stunned and silent party by small launch to Grasnaya where we were welcomed and settled in the Mess.'

The funeral had to be arranged immediately. It took place at midday on 27 September 1942 in a Russian cemetery in the hills above Vaenga airfield, in the sector set aside for those members of the British forces whose lives had been lost when rendering aid to our Russian allies. It was attended by all members of 210 Squadron still at Grasnaya, as well as by Wing Commander Sandeman, who had taken over command of all our forces from Group Captain Hobbs at the close of Operation 'Orator'. George Adamson's diary records the solemnity and tranquility of the occasion:

'On the Monday was Tim's funeral. We all went in open lorry to Vaenga, some six miles away, as many RAF men as could and George the Russki interpreter. At the hospital we collected the coffin; it was put on a small lorry draped with a Union Jack; followed by a Russian guard of honour, eight of us as coffin bearers, and then the rest of the mourners. We marched slowly up the hill behind the lumbering bearer. It was a brilliant and beautiful afternoon, practically without cloud, and the sun giving glow to every fading birch leaf and twinkle to the granite that pushed here and there through the lichen and grass. When the road became impossible we carried Tim's body to the grave.

The Winco said "Our Father" and a volley of shots was fired; he saluted and then the company in turn. (Alas, they could do no better and had no prayer book; I said a De Profundis for the repose of his soul.)'

As we walked down from the cemetery, in the silence and the crisp cold air, all of us thought of what we had done together, but the phrase 'on one's own' would have to take on a different meaning. However, as so often happened in wartime, personal tragedy was not allowed to delay events. We were airborne again on 27 September on our way back to the Shetlands, to carry on the war effort elsewhere. I was a passenger on Catalina 'Q', captained by Flight Lieutenant J.A. Holmes DFC. It was the only occasion I slept in a Catalina, not on one of the bunks but crouched in the navigator's compartment, with knees bent over the duckboard.

This chance encounter of two reconnaissance aircraft over the vast expanse of the Barents Sea had resulted in the loss to the RAF of 'Tim' Healy but the Catalina was repaired and flown home. The enemy lost one aircraft and its crew of four. If we had known of the German loss in 1942, we would probably have felt exhilarated, but today we can only reflect with sadness on the distress to the next-of-kin and the desolation of war.

*

This book has been written for two reasons. One is that it may make a small contribution to the history of the RAF, for it covers a series of episodes that have attracted little attention. The other is to commemorate the achievements of one of the RAF's finest young officers, Flight Lieutenant D.E. 'Tim' Healy. It was a privilege to have shared in his aspirations and to have experienced the superb team spirit which developed under his leadership. In the Air Forces Museum at Runnymede, he is recorded as follows:

Healy, Flt Lieut. Dennis Edward, 60287, DSO, Norwegian War Cross. RAF 210 Squadron, 25th September 1942. Age 27. Son of Henry Francis and Maud Healy, husband of Hazel Madeline Healy of Stanmore, Middx. Panel 65.

Epilogue

After completing my tour with Coastal Command, I became an instructor on Staff Navigation courses at No 47 Air School at Queenstown in South Africa, part of the Commonwealth Air Training Scheme. On my return to the UK in April 1945, I asked for a posting to the Empire Air Navigation School in Shropshire, which was the most senior navigation establishment in the RAF and often regarded as a general university of the air.

If my request had been granted, I would have joined the unit a few days before Wing Commander D.C. McKinley, DFC, AFC, took off from Shawbury for Iceland, in order to begin a series of polar flights in the Avro Lancaster 'Aries'. The purpose of these flights was to investigate problems of air navigation in high latitude and polar navigation. Special charts and techniques of air navigation had been devised. A variety of instruments, including automatic dead-reckoning gear, were to be tried out. A magnetic survey in the region of the North Magnetic Pole was to be made, and the behaviour of magnetic compasses examined. Other intentions were to collect meteorological, engine and airframe data, to test the possibility of mapping icefields by radar, to take photographs of Arctic topography, and to study the effects of polar flying on aircrew efficiency.

Several modifications to the Lancaster bomber had been made for these flights. Heavy gun turrets and armour plating had been removed. The nose and tail had been streamlined and the camouflage replaced by aluminium paint. Four new Rolls Royce Merlin XXIV engines had been fitted. A variety of instruments not normally carried on service aircraft, including eleven different types of magnetic compasses, were brought into use. Since magnetic compasses could not be relied upon in the region of the North Magnetic Pole, a second astrodome was fitted; it was estimated that about 60 astro sights would be needed on the 600 mile journey between Peary Land and the North Geographical Pole.

Oxygen equipment was made available for all the crew, so that the aircraft could fly above the weather. Adequate heating had been installed in the pilots' cockpit, although not extended into the remainder of the fuselage. No cooking facilities for food were available, but there were plenty of sandwiches, together with fruit and hot drinks. For emergency use, enough equipment was provided to maintain the party on the polar ice for four weeks. This included special clothing, food, cooking equipment, snow shoes, ice axes, rifles, fishing tackle and portable radio transmitter/receivers.

However, it has to be remembered that in 1945 such sophisticated instruments as inertia navigation had not been fully developed, and that air navigation was still dependent on human endeavour, skill and judgment. For this reason, there was assembled on the 'Aries' a concentration of men whose personal prowess must have been without precedent in the RAF. There were four pilots, one of whom was also a medical officer, as well as four officers with the specialist navigational qualifications provided by the Empire Air Navigation School at Shawbury. Wing Commander K.C. Maclure, AFC, was the senior officer responsible for conducting research, collecting magnetic readings and other special data. The senior navigator responsible for collecting all external observations for handing to the navigation-plotter was Wing Commander E.W. Anderson, OBE, DFC. The navigation-plotter was Flight Lieutenant S.T. Underwood, whose job was to maintain a continuous record of the path of the aircraft. Squadron Leader A.J. Hagger was the second pilot, as well as the meteorological observer and photographer. Wing Commander R.H. Winfield, DFC, AFC, was the pilot/medical officer, with the function of assisting the senior observer. The crew was completed by Flying Officer S. Blakley and Warrant Officer A.F. Smith as wireless operators, Corporal W.S. Gardner as rigger, and Leading Aircraftmen E. Wiggins and H.B. Dean as fitter/electricians.

The first flight made by the 'Aries' was to be to the North Pole. The aircraft took off from Meeks Field at Reykjavik, the capital of Iceland, at 03.00 hours on 16 May 1945. The crew climbed to the operational height of 15,000 feet and headed northwards. The intended track lay along the eastern coast of Greenland, similar to the route of our attempt on 22 August 1942. The crew were unable to enjoy the splendour of the massive stretch of mountains and solid ice, however, for this was covered by a thickening bank of cloud. This brought the danger of icing and a reduction in the range of the aircraft. They tried to edge round it to the east, but without success.

Similarly, they were unable to climb above it, and were thus unable to take astro sights. Like us in Tim Healy's crew, they had no alternative but to turn back. They arrived back at Reykjavik after an abortive flight of nine hours.

Weather reports indicated that clearer weather could be expected further to the east. One of the problems was that there was only a short period in the middle of the month when the sun and the moon were in suitable positions for 'fixes' of astro positions to be calculated. The crew could not afford to wait and, after only a couple of hours' rest, they set off again. This time, they headed towards Jan Mayen Island before turning northwards. The forecast proved to be correct. The different route enabled the crew to defeat the elements and to achieve their objective. They arrived back at Reykjavik at 09.00 hours on 17 May, having flown over the North Pole about seven hours earlier.

On the next occasion, they flew to the North Magnetic Pole and landed in northern Canada. Finally, they moved on to north-western Canada and flew back to Shawbury by a route which took them over the North Magnetic Pole once more.

Navigation by the 'Greenwich Grid System' proved to be fully effective on these flights. Radio instruments functioned perfectly, and the specially adapted magnetic compasses indicated magnetic north even when the aircraft was over the North Pole, about 600 miles away. The crew collected a mass of data to be analysed on their return to Shawbury.

With so little recorded information about Arctic flying to guide them, it was a step into the unknown for the crew of the 'Aries'. Looking back at these events from an era when high latitude flying by scheduled airlines has become commonplace, it is difficult to place in perspective the effort and determination that was needed to ensure such complete success. The Air Officer C-in-C Flying Training Command and the Commandant of the Empire Air Navigation School, who welcomed the crew back to Shawbury on 26 May 1945, had good cause to praise the quality of their performance. The navigational success of the expedition was rightly regarded as another triumph for the School.

APPENDICES

Correspondence with Headquarters, Coastal Command *

From:– Headquarters, Coastal Command
To:– Air Officer Commanding, No 18 Group

MOST

Date:– 24th April, 1942   *SECRET*
Ref:– CC/S.7010/H/PLANS

Ice Reconnaissance

1.   In confirmation of telephone conversation with Group Captain DICKEN of this headquarters, one Catalina and crew is to be detailed for ice reconnaissance work. Catalina W8428 fitted with long-range ASV and DR compass is to be allotted to No 210 Squadron under your command. The aircraft is to be collected from RAF Station GREENOCK where it will be ready to fly on 28th April.

2.   The aircraft will be required to operate in the first instance from SULLOM VOE.

3.   The first operation of this aircraft is an ice reconnaissance to BEAR ISLAND, SPITSBERGEN, ISFJORD†, and along the ice edge to JAN MAYEN ISLAND landing at REYKJAVIK. The flight is to take place on 29th April or as soon after as possible.

4.   Lieutenant Colonel GODFREY and Lieutenant GLEN will be taken as ice observers on the flight and you are requested to confirm arrangements made for the transport of these two officers from INVERGORDON to SULLOM VOE, to Group Captain DICKEN of this Headquarters.

5.   You are requested to confirm also the date of arrival of the Catalina at SULLOM VOE and the estimated time and date of departure of the flight. The two passengers will travel by night train from LONDON to INVERGORDON.

6.   On the successful completion of this flight, the aircraft is to return to SULLOM VOE and prepare for extensive ice reconnaissance

* Public Record Office papers AIR 15 211.
† Coastal Command used the Norwegian spelling of ICEFJORD.

flights commencing about the middle of May, and operating from SPITSBERGEN.

7.   Two reconnaissance flights are required from SPITSBERGEN, as follows:–

(a)   ISFJORD, SPITSBERGEN – North East GREENLAND – North Pole – Cape LEIGH SMITH, North East Land – ISJFORD, SPITSBERGEN: approximately 1,800 miles.

(b)   ISFJORD, SPITSBERGEN – RUDOLF Island, FRIDHJOF NANSEN LAND, Cape ZHELANIYA, NOVAYA ZEMLYA – southwards to the open water and thence following the edge of the drift ice westwards to SPITSBERGEN: approximately 1,500 miles.

8.   Arrangements will be made for the crew to discuss these flights in LONDON with Admiral RISER LARSEN and Commodore LUTZOW-HOLN* who are experienced in Polar flying.

9.   Details of the arrangements made regarding maintenance, fuel, charts, polar equipment and meteorological information will be communicated to you as soon as possible.

> G.B.A. Baker, Air Vice Marshal.
> for
> AIR CHIEF MARSHAL,
> Commanding-in-Chief,
> COASTAL COMMAND.

From:–   A.S.T. Godfrey, Lieutenant Colonel
To:–   Group Captain C.W. Dicken, Headquarters, Coastal Command
Date:–   5th May 1942

> At Akureyri, Iceland

Dear Group Captain,

Though we have not met I feel I should drop you a line following the trip to Spitsbergen on which I was an ice observer with Glen.

As a layman I should have thought that the achievement of Flight Lieutenant Healy was a finer one than the last trip to Spits. He and his crew had a tricky time and were superb.

I think the most thorough ice recce has been done. The organisation at Sullom was grand and it is good to know that this trip is being followed by a captain and crew who are so interested in the business and absolutely on top line.

* Correct spelling should have been Admiral Riiser-Larsen and Commodore Lutzow-Holm.

The Catalina is taking back the ice report.

> Yours sincerely,
> A.S.T. Godfrey, Lt Col.

From:–   A.R. Glen, Lieutenant Commander
To:–   Group Captain C.W. Dicken, Headquarters, Coastal Command.
Date:–   5th May 1942

> Akureyri, Iceland

My dear Dicken,

Just a short note to tell you what a splendid trip we had and how excellent were Healy and his crew. They are certainly the perfect crew for the future flights and there is not one weak member amongst them. Healy especially is first class and deserves the fullest recognition for the job which he did.

The island itself was unfortunately fogbound with visibility less than 100 yards and the fog right down to the deck. There could have been no question of landing as the air temperature was down to minus 20 and the boat would have become too heavily coated with ice. We tried to follow the coast but it was too dangerous so we had to turn back somewhere between Hornsund and Bellsund. However elsewhere the weather was very nearly perfect and we made the most detailed ice reconnaissance between Bear Island and Spitsbergen as well as from Spits to Jan Mayen. The results were unexpected and I believe extremely important. Instruments did not function too well and I cannot over-emphasise the excellence of the navigation. Spits itself was just sheer bad luck, a day which one would never expect to find in May or June.

I believe the future flights will tie up the whole problem and I do want to stress the confidence I feel in Healy. I also want to thank you most sincerely for all you have done. I only wish you may find it possible to come and spend some time with us in the north.

> Yours ever,
> Sandy R. Glen

The Flight Made by Flight Lieutenant G.G. Potier

A copy of the log kept by the navigator, Pilot Officer R.J. Fairley, was published in Appendix A of Volume 5 of the Coastal Command Navigation Review, and is still available to researchers at the Air Historical Branch of the Ministry of Defence. The accompanying article in the Review included these comments:

> The sortie, a reconnaissance of Spitsbergen, lasted for 23 hours, covered a distance of 2,325 nautical miles, and was successfully completed up to 78 degrees North, using both P9 and P4 compasses as the DR compass was unserviceable . . .
>
> These figures (the analysed results of the flight) are highly commendable. In addition, the navigation log is evidence of steady work on the part of its author. Not many of us would care to spend the best part of a day inside the Arctic Circle, and it is nice to know that the Heinkel in Icefjord never flew again. . . .*
>
> Far be it for us to be armchair critics, but we beg leave to draw lessons from this sample of navigation which may be of benefit to all of us, without decrying what was a very stout effort. First and foremost there is a much too frequent use of the Drift and Wind Lane method of finding the wind. This is particularly dangerous when the course is doubtful, since the plotting of the correct course, track and wind lanes must be above suspicion if an accurate wind is required. Unless the wind is almost abeam, even small inaccuracies of the three directions will produce phoney answers.
>
> The navigator was not concerned with track crawling, but many of the drifts taken do not seem to have been used. No indication of their reliability is given by saying how they were obtained. The details of one of the two astro sights are not recorded, although it might have been wished to refer to them at a

---

* In fact, the Germans were able to fly the Heinkel back to Banak.

later stage. The astro compass was also sparingly used considering the ineffectiveness of the magnetic compass at these latitudes. There is no indication of the weather conditions encountered. No doubt the old log form employed did not encourage clarity, and the reluctance to give ETAs may in part also be attributed to its use. We feel that the log would have been more readable, even to the navigator himself, if he had refrained from repeating tracks, courses, etc., whenever making an entry without changing course. But this is only a matter of personal opinion.

This 'personal opinion' aroused scornful responses in the navigation room of 210 Squadron, in spite of its authoritative source. The critic was correct in saying that Dick Fairley was not track-crawling, but the presumption that the 'air pilot' method of navigation was being used on a high-latitude flight indicated how much he was out of touch with squadron practice. When using Mercator charts, the increasing rate of change of scale in high latitudes made the 'air pilot' method of navigation unsuitable for long flights, particularly in north–south directions; it could give rise to errors in the aircraft, where the environment was far less favourable than the peaceful conditions of a navigation office.

It is probable that Dick Fairley did not record the reliability of the readings in his log because he had rejected those which were unreliable. He would certainly have used his judgement about them. All the drifts he had recorded had been used, to plot accurate tracks and to measure wind velocity so that ground speed and distances could be calculated. We were aware that track plotting and the 'drift and wind lane' method of finding wind velocity were not approved officially, but we also knew how accurately this method could be used by an experienced navigator when flying at low level.

The actual landfalls achieved provided clear proof of the excellent quality of the navigation on this long flight. The 'track plot' which Dick Fairley had carried out in the air was probably at least the equal in accuracy of the 'air pilot' which his critics had completed on the ground.

Polar Navigation

'Why,' said the Dodo, 'the best way to explain it is to do it.'

Alice in Wonderland

This Appendix is a summary of the techniques which the crew of 'P for Peter' of 210 Squadron intended to use when flying beyond the 80th parallel of latitude to the North Pole. Since the flight had to be abandoned before reaching that latitude, the methods were not put into practice. This summary assumes that the reader has a knowledge of the normal procedures of astro navigation in aircraft, in lower latitudes.*

Chart
A 'Polar Zenithal Equidistant' chart had been prepared under the guidance of Professor Debenham at Cambridge University. This was on a scale of one inch equal to 30 nautical miles. Thus the 600 nautical miles from the 80th parallel to the North Pole were represented on the chart by 20 inches. This was a very convenient size for use on the navigation table in the Catalina.†

Direction
When viewed from the North Pole, all directions point southwards, so that a different method of describing direction was needed for polar navigation. An obvious solution was to make use of the concept of Greenwich Hour Angle (GHA) used in astro navigation to describe the angular difference from the celestial meridian of Greenwich to that of a heavenly body such as the sun, measured in a westerly direction. The datum line then became the direction of Greenwich as viewed from the North Pole, namely the Greenwich

---

* For practical experience of polar navigation, there is a summary of the Aries flights in *The Geographical Journal* Vol 107 of 1946.
† See page 230 for an impression of this chart.

Meridian from the Pole. From that direction, there could be a 360 degree clockwise rotation, as for GHA. Such a method could be used over the whole of the polar area, the datum line from the observer always being drawn parallel to the Greenwich Meridian. To avoid confusion with astro terminology, such directions were described in degrees 'G' rather than 'GHA'.

On a polar flight, all directions (wind velocities as well as aircraft courses and tracks) would be measured in degrees 'G'. It was intended to plot tracks on the polar chart, using the Dalton Navigational Computor Mark III as effectively in terms of degrees 'G' as for degrees 'T' ('T' being the generally accepted symbol to represent true directions in relation to the North Pole).

An added advantage of this system of direction notation for polar flying was the simplicity of the conversion formula between degrees 'T' and degrees 'G':

Degrees 'G' = Degrees 'T' + 180 + longitude west or − longitude east.

Astro Compass

The astro compass, using the sun as the arbiter of direction, was expected to be the most reliable guide for navigational purposes. For parts of the polar flight, it might be the only guide. There were two ways in which it could be used.

The first method treated the compass as a model of the celestial sphere, with settings for the declination and hour angle of the sun and for the latitude of the observer, account having been taken of his longitude in arriving at hour angle. However, on a polar flight, a small error in the dead-reckoning position could cause a large error in the hour angle setting and a corresponding error in the aircraft heading indicated by the lubber line on the compass. Accurate navigation was dependent upon accurate courses; it was undesirable to have accurate courses dependent upon accurate navigation.

The second method, which we intended to use, overcame this difficulty. It treated the astro compass as a bearing plate, without needing any settings for latitude and longitude. At the North Pole, the sun is above the horizon all day long during the summer months, although of course it can be obscured by inclement weather. There, the direction of the sun in terms of degrees 'G' is the same as its GHA, the latter being recorded in the Air Almanac against Greenwich Mean Time (GMT). Thus, at the North Pole, the astro compass, used as a bearing plate, could readily indicate the course of the aircraft (in degrees 'G') by the angular difference between the direction of the sun (shown by a shadow against the compass marker) and the fore and aft line of the aircraft (shown by the lubber line).

When the aircraft was 600 miles from the North Pole, the direction (or azimuth) of the sun, in degrees 'G', would differ from its GHA, but by no more than four degrees. It was intended, therefore, that we should use the astro compass *throughout the whole* of the polar flight and make adjustments for the small differences between the sun's azimuth and its GHA by means of a simple guide called a 'GHA to G Correction Chart'.*

There were four mountings for the astro compass in 'P for Peter', one outside each of the pilots' windows and one inside each blister cupola. The window or the cupola had to be opened in order to use the compass, and care had to be taken not to drop the instrument when fitting it to the mounting, even though we carried a spare. When the sun was in front of the mainplane, the pilot on the sunny side would be responsible for making the relevant settings and maintaining courses from the readings. Since the sun's GHA changes by one degree every four minutes, the azimuth setting would require regular adjustment. When the sun was abaft the mainplane, the compass would have been mounted in one of the blister cupolas, alongside the gun mounting. Then corrections of course would have to be given over the intercom. Between these compass readings, the pilots would maintain direction by reference to one of the magnetic compasses or the directional gyroscope.

Magnetic Compasses

'P for Peter' was fitted with three compasses suitable for polar navigation. The distant-reading gyro-magnetic compass was expected to be serviceable as far as 85 degrees North. There were also specially balanced P9 and P4 compasses. A 'high-latitude P9 compass' had been used for the campaign in Narvik, where the horizontal strength of the earth's magnetic field was lower than in more southerly latitudes. A 'double-high-latitude P4 compass' had been designed to cope with the Spitsbergen area, where the horizontal force was even lower. Both these compasses were expected to be serviceable to at least 85 degrees North, and possibly

* See page 231 for this chart.

beyond that latitude.

Varigees and Isogogees

In air navigation, the deflection of a compass needle from True North towards Magnetic North is described as 'variation'. Lines drawn on a chart joining places of equal magnetic variation are known as 'isogonals'. To make use of magnetic compasses in polar navigation, a technique had to be devised to allow for the difference between the direction of Magnetic North and the datum line in terms of Degrees 'G'. To avoid confusion, some special terminology was needed. A term corresponding to 'variation' could be 'varigee', while lines drawn on a chart joining places of equal varigee could be 'isogogees'. Once marked on the chart, the isogogees would give a readily available indication, at all stages along the aircraft's track, of the relationship between the compass heading in degrees magnetic and the aircraft heading in degrees 'G'.

Marking isogogees on a polar chart called for some inspired guess-work. An article in *The Geographical Journal* by Harold Spencer Jones (later to become the Astronomer Royal) and one in *The American Geophysical Journal* by Harlan W. Fisk were studied. They gave different estimates of the lie of isogonals in the polar area, but they presented a similar pattern. Both indicated that variation was expected to change by not more than ten degrees between 80 and 87 degrees North latitude along the 20 degree West meridian.

With this guidance, estimated isogonals were plotted on the polar chart. By applying the conversion formula at various points along the isogonals and marking suitable interpolations, corresponding isogogees were plotted for the area between north-east Greenland and the North Pole. The resulting graticule indicated that, to maintain a constant direction in degrees 'G' between 80 and 85 degrees North latitude along the meridian of 20 degrees West, it would be necessary to make only gradual adjustments to the magnetic course.

This preoccupation with varigees and isogogees was no more than a precautionary measure in case the sun became hidden by inclement weather on our return journey. We intended to place reliance on the astro compass, but to make use of magnetic compasses to maintain steady course between astro readings. The serviceability of the magnetic compasses and the accuracy of the estimated isogogees were among the various checks to be made on the outward journey.

POLAR ZENITHAL EQUIDISTANT CHART

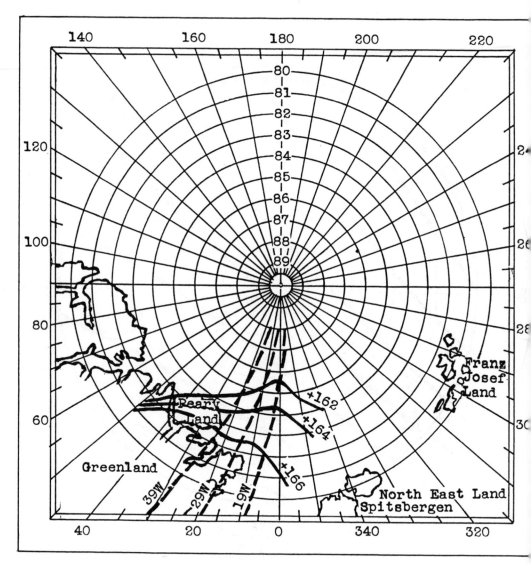

Chart showing estimates made in 1942 of isogonals (e.g. 19°W) and 'isogogees' (e.g. +166°) to convert magnetic headings into directions in terms of degrees 'True' or degrees 'G' as far as 85 degrees North latitude. It was intended to check their accuracy by use of the astro compass during the flight.

'GHA' TO 'G' CORRECTION CHART
Correction Curves for Declination 20° North

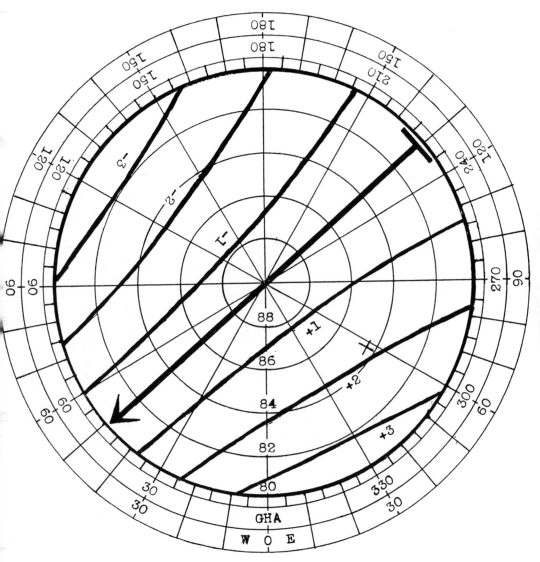

Example:
DR position: 84°30' North 58°10' East
GHA Sun: 049°
1. Rotate card to set arrow against 049° on GHA scale.
2. Read correction to be applied for that position (+2°).
3. Azimuth of sun is 049° + 2° = 051°G.

Astro Navigation

In addition to using the sun as a direction indicator, it was intended to take frequent sextant observation of the sun's altitude above the horizontal, in order to plot position lines on the chart. Because of the proximity of the aircraft to the North Pole, there was a quick and reasonably accurate method of doing this, which involved far less calculation than in the astro navigation in more southerly latitudes.

At the North Pole itself, the corrected observed altitude of the sun would be equal to its declination. Away from the North Pole, the distance of the observer from the Pole would be equal to the difference between the sun's altitude and its declination (one minute of arc being equal to one nautical mile). If the sun's altitude were less than its declination, the resulting minus sign would indicate that the position line was on the side of the Pole away from the sun.

The corrected observed altitude of the sun provided the navigator with a circle of position at right angles to the sun's azimuth. But the latter was readily available from the GHA markings (equal to degrees 'G') around the perimeter of the chart. The quick method required the observer simply to deduct the sun's declination from the corrected observed altitude in terms of minutes of arc, and then to mark off that distance in nautical miles from the Pole along the sun's meridian (or anti-meridian). At that marker, he then drew a line on the chart at right angles to the meridian. That line would be a tangent to the circle of position. When the aircraft was close to the Pole, the tangent could be regarded as coincidental to the circle of position. When the aircraft was 300 miles from the sun's meridian, the difference between the tangent and the arc of the position line would give an error of about five miles; when 600 miles away, the error could be up to twenty miles. Speed of operation was likely to be more important than meticulous accuracy and, where appropriate, a rule of thumb adjustment could be made.

If the limit of endurance had permitted (as it would have done from a base in Spitsbergen), the aim would have been to fly to one side of the Pole until corrected observed altitude was equal to the sun's declination. 'P for Peter' would then have reached a circle of equal altitude which also passed over the North Pole. Course would then have been altered to fly at right angles to the sun's azimuth, so that the Catalina could run along the position line until it passed over the Pole. After a suitable time interval, another 90 degree turn would have set us on our homeward journey. This technique was also used by the Aries in 1945.

It was intended to plan the flight so that the sun would be ahead of or behind the aircraft as the Pole was approached, so that the sextant observation of the sun's altitude would have given the required latitude check. Six hours later, when approaching the 80th parallel on the return journey, a sun sight would have given a position line running in a north–south direction, to guide us to the required landfall at north–east Greenland. For the crew of 'P for Peter', polar navigation would then have ceased and normal high-latitude navigation would have been resumed.

Decorations

Norwegian Forces:

Captain E. Ullring	Distinguished Service Order Norwegian War Cross (with sword) Norwegian War Medal Russian War Medal
Lieutenant-Colonel E. Sverdrup	Norwegian War Cross (Posthumous)
Captain O.R. Lund	Distinguished Service Cross Norwegian War Cross
Captain Ross	Member of the British Empire
Lieutenant P. Henningstad	Norwegian War Medal
Lieutenant K. Knudsen	Norwegian War Medal
2nd Lieutenant A.F. Forseth	Norwegian War Medal
Lieutentant H. Øi	Norwegian War Medal
Lieutenant A. Pedersen	Norwegian War Medal
Sergeant R. Knutsen	Military Medal Norwegian War Medal
Corporal Ostbye	Military Medal
Able Seaman Nils Langbak	Distinguished Service Medal Norwegian War Medal
Private Mellerby	Military Medal
Private Skoglund	Norwegian War Medal
Private Thorvik	Norwegian War Medal
Rating E.J. Sannes	Norwegian War Medal

Royal Navy:

Lieutenant Commander A.R. Glen	Distinguished Service Cross Norwegian War Cross (with sword)

British Army:

Lieutenant-Colonel A.S.T. Godfrey	Norwegian Military Cross (Posthumous)
Major A.B. Whatman	Member of the British Empire Norwegian War Cross

Royal Air Force:

Wing Commander H.B. Johnson	Distinguished Flying Cross Norwegian War Medal
Flight Lieutenant D.E. Hawkins	Distinguished Flying Cross
Flight Lieutenant D.E. Healy	Distinguished Service Order Norwegian War Cross
Flight Lieutenant J.A.Holmes	Distinguished Flying Cross
Flight Lieutenant B. Lewin	Distinguished Flying Cross
Flight Lieutenant G.G. Potier	Distinguished Flying Cross
Pilot Officer E. Schofield	Distinguished Flying Cross
Pilot Officer J.G. Wright	Distinguished Flying Cross
Sergeant T.R. Thomas	Norwegian War Medal
Sergeant G.V. Kingett	Distinguished Flying Medal

BIBLIOGRAPHY AND SOURCES

Bibliography and Sources

Elbo, J.G. 'The War in Svalbard 1939–45.' *The Polar Record* Vol 6. Cambridge: The Scott Polar Research Institute, 1952.

Glen, A.R. *Footholds against a Whirlwind*. London: Hutchinson, 1975.

Joubert, Sir Phillip & Glen, A.R. 'High Latitude Flying by Coastal Command in suport of convoys to north Russia.' *The Geographical Journal* Vol 108. London: The Royal Geographical Society, 1946.

Hinsley, F.H. *British Intelligence in the Second World War*, Vol III, Part I. London: HMSO, 1984.

Lindsay, M. *Three Got Through*. London: Falcon, 1946.

McKinley, D.C. 'The Arctic Flights of Aries.' *The Geographical Journal* Vol 107. London: The Royal Geographical Society, 1946.

Maclure, K.C. 'Technical Aspects of the Aries Flights.' *The Geographical Journal* Vol 107. London: The Royal Geographical Society, 1946.

Schwerdtfeger, W. & Selinger, F. *Wetterflieger in der Arktis 1940–1944*. Stuttgart: Motorbuch Verlag, 1982.

Selinger, F. & Glen, A. 'Arctic Meteorological Operations and Counter Operations during World War II.' *The Polar Record* Vol 21. Cambridge: The Scott Polar Research Institute, 1983.

Terraine, J. *The Right of the Line – The Royal Air Force in the European War 1939–1945*. London: Hodder & Stoughton, 1985.

Winfield, R. 'Notes on the Medical Aspects of the Aries Flights.' *The Geographical Journal* Vol 107. London: the Royal Geographical Society, 1946.

Winfield, R. *The Royal Air Force North Polar Research Flights 1945*. The Polar Record Vol 5. Cambridge: The Scott Polar Research Institute, 1947.

Public Record Office:

ADM1	11962	1942	Report on proceedings by Captain Ullring, Royal Norwegian Navy: Operation Gearbox. Activities of landing party operating in the Svalbard, Barentsberg area of Norway.
ADM1	12397	1942 1943	Honours and Awards, Operations Fritham and Gearbox (Expedition to Spitsbergen). Lt Cmdr Glen awarded Norwegian War Cross with Sword.
ADM1	12398	1942 1943	Honours and Awards, Operations Fritham and Gearbox (Expedition to Spitsbergen). Able

Seaman Nils Landback, R. awarded DSM.

ADM199	448	1942 1943	Naval Operations in Europe – HM Ships: reports of proceedings, Operation Gearbox.	
ADM199	730	1940 1945	Various operations – reports, Operation Fritham.	
ADM199	758	1942 1943	PQ and QP convoys; reports; Operation Gearbox II; reports.	
AIR2	4911	1942 1952	Proposed award for Polar Medal. Spitsbergen flights.	
AIR2	8468	1942	June 11–July 31. Immediate awards.	
AIR15	211	1942	Mar–July. Spitsbergen Reconnaissances.	
AIR15	227	1941 1943	Operational control of Coastal Command by Admiralty.	
AIR15	380	1942	Aug–Nov. Operation Orator.	
AIR15	381	1942	Oct–Nov. Operation Orator; reports.	
AIR15	382	1942	Sep. Convoys PQ18 & QP14: Narrative of Air Operations.	
AIR15	456	1940	Jan–1947 Dec.	Flying Boats. Air Staff Policy.
AIR15	470	1942	Jan–1943 Apl.	*Coastal Command Review* Vol I Spitsbergen, Oct 1942 A Coastal Command Expedition to Russia, Nov 1942.
AIR15	472	1944	Jan–1944 Dec.	*Coastal Command Review* Vol III Ocean Landings by Flying Boats, Jan 1944.
AIR15	488	1941	Aug–1943 Jun.	Role and Employment of Catalina aircraft.
AIR15	537	1941	Sep–1946 Feb.	No 18 Group Operational Role.
AIR15	602	1942		Polar Navigation Papers.
AIR27	1184	1943	Jan–1943 Dec.	No 202 Squadron Operations Record Book.
AIR27	1299	1941	Jan–1943 Dec.	No 210 Squadron Operations Record Book.
AIR28	775	1940	Jan–1943 Dec.	Sullom Voe (Shetlands) Operations Record Book.

AIR40   1997   1942 May–1942 Aug.   Spitsbergen: reports on ice
                                        conditions, airfields and
                                        weather.

AIR41   47   Undated.   *The RAF in Maritime War – The Atlantic
                             and Home Waters*, Vol III, Chapter VIII,
                             Part II. Reconnaissance and Operations
                             over Spitsbergen.

INDEX

Index